@Copyright 2019by Kayla Jelley- **All rights reserved.**

This document is geared towards providing exact and reliable information in regards to the topic and issue covered. The publication is sold with the idea that the publisher is not required to render accounting, officially permitted, or otherwise, qualified services. If advice is necessary, legal or professional, a practiced individual in the profession should be ordered.

Under no circumstance will any legal responsibility or blame be held against the publisher for any reparation, damages, or monetary loss due to the information herein, either directly or indirectly.

Legal Notice: The book is copyright protected. This is only for personal use. You cannot amend, distribute, sell, use, quote or paraphrase any part or the content within this book without the consent of the author.

Disclaimer Notice: Please note the information contained within this document is for educational and entertainment purposes only. Every attempt has been made to provide accurate, up to date and reliable complete information. No warranties of any kind are expressed or implied. Readers acknowledge that the author is not engaging in the rendering of legal, financial, medical or professional advice. The content of this book has been derived from various sources. Please consult a licensed professional before attempting any techniques outlined in this book.

CONTENTS

Introduction 8

Chapter-1: Understanding the Mediterranean Diet 8

    What is the Mediterranean Diet? 8

    The History of the Mediterranean Diet 9

    The Science behind the Mediterranean Diet 9

Chapter-2: Living healthier and longer on the Mediterranean Diet 12

    The Incredible Health Benefits of Eating the Mediterranean Way 12

    A Delicious Path to Weight Loss 13

Chapter-3: Starting the Mediterranean Diet 14

    Planning your Mediterranean Diet 14

    The Top 10 tips for Success 15

Chapter-4 Eating on the Mediterranean Diet 17

    What's on your Plate? 17

    Your Mediterranean Shopping Diet 18

    Eating Out on the Mediterranean diet 19

    Seven-Day Sample Meal Plan 20

Breakfast Recipes 23

    Pina Colada Smoothie 23

    Green Poached Egg Toasts 23

    Kiwi Smoothie 24

    Soufflé Omelet with Mushrooms 25

Spinach Parmesan Baked Eggs 26

Red smoothie 26

Sweet Potato Breakfast Hash 27

Spinach and Feta Baked Egg 28

Mediterranean Smoothie 29

Small Plates and Snacks Recipes 29

Niçoise toasts 29

Herbed Olives 30

Stuffed tomatoes 31

Crispy Squid with Capers 32

Spiced Tortilla 33

Crustless Vegetable Quiche 33

Ditalini Minestrone 35

Baked Kale and Eggs with Ricotta 36

Ham and Poached Egg English Muffin 36

Salads and Soups Recipes 37

Red Barley Soup 37

Mediterranean Sardine Salad 38

Greek Meatball Soup 39

Aubergine and Pepper Salad 40

Zucchini Soup 41

Black Beans Feta Salad 42

Napoletana Hoki Soup 42

Chickpeas Pepper Salad 43

Passata Cream Soup..44

Beans, Rice and Grains Recipes...45

Spinach Beans..45

Meatballs Chickpea Medley..46

Lemony Mushroom and Herb Rice..47

Citrus Garlic Beans..47

Cashew Rice...48

Moroccan Couscous..49

Greek Stock Beans..50

Baked Mediterranean Rice...51

Bean Mash with Grilled Veggies..51

Sandwiches and Wraps Recipes...52

Avocado and Egg Sandwich...52

Mediterranean Veggie Wrap..53

Loaded Mediterranean Veggie Sandwich...54

Couscous and Chicken Tender Wrap..55

Mediterranean Grilled Cheese Sandwich...55

Mediterranean Fish Wraps...56

Pita Sandwich...57

Mushroom Veggies Wrap...58

Mediterranean Pressed Sandwich..59

Pizza and Pasta Recipes..59

Garlic Bread Pizzas..59

Mediterranean Olive Oil Pasta...60

Easy Tomato Pizzas 61

Mediterranean Whole Wheat Pasta 62

Goat's Cheese Pizza 63

Pasta with Sautéed Spinach and Garlic 64

Mediterranean Artichoke Pizza 64

Mediterranean Cauliflower Pizza 65

Margherita Pizza 66

Fish and Seafood Recipes 67

Mixed Seafood Stew 67

Sauce Dipped Mussels 68

Squid Oyster Medley 69

Crusty Grilled Mussels 70

Seafood Garlic Couscous 71

Lobster Rice Paella 72

Fish and Vegetable Parcels 73

Seafood with Couscous Salad 74

Saffron Fish Gratins 75

Vegetable Main Dishes Recipes 76

Griddled Vegetable and Feta Tart 76

Mediterranean Gnocchi 76

Parmesan Roasted Broccoli 77

Baked Goat Cheese with Tomato Sauce 78

Roasted Vegetable Tabbouleh 79

Vegan Pesto Spaghetti Squash 80

    Smoky Roasted Vegetables 80

    Baked Goat Cheese with Tomato Sauce 81

    Charred Green Beans with Mustard 82

Chicken Recipes 83

    Mediterranean Chicken and Orzo 83

    Greek Chicken with Roasted Spring Vegetables 84

    Chicken with Tomato Sauce 85

    Hasselback Caprese Chicken 86

    Mediterranean Chicken Quinoa Bowl 87

    Olive Chicken 88

    Roasted Mediterranean Chicken 89

    Lemon-Thyme Chicken 90

    Mediterranean Chicken with Potatoes 91

Meat Recipes 92

    Mediterranean Beef Pinwheels 92

    Pork Tenderloin with Orzo 93

    Vegetables Lamb Shanks 94

    Greek Beef Steak and Hummus Plate 95

    Garlic and Rosemary Mediterranean Pork Roast 96

    Baked Lamb Tray 97

    Mediterranean Beef Kofta 97

    Blue Cheese-Topped Pork Chops 98

    Lamb Pasta and Cheese 99

Dessert Recipes 100

Banana Greek Yogurt Bowl.. 100

Greek Baklava.. 101

Popped Quinoa Bars.. 102

Honey yogurt cheesecake... 102

Orange Sesame Cookies.. 103

Almond Orange Pandoro.. 104

Fruity Almond cake... 105

Honey Glazed Pears.. 106

Compote Dipped Berries Mix...107

Introduction

The Mediterranean diet is based upon the culture and cuisines of the Mediterranean region. Numerous scientific and medical studies have argued and proven that the Mediterranean diet is very healthy and is a perfect diet plan for avoiding various chronic diseases, such as cancer and cardiac complications. It is especially beneficial because it boosts life expectancy.

Chapter-1: Understanding the Mediterranean Diet

What is the Mediterranean Diet?

The Mediterranean diet plan has various specific characteristics, which make it different from other diet plans. These include the following:

1. The significant portion of the diet plan is derived from multiple plant-related sources, such as bread, rice, fruits, legumes (lentils and beans), whole grains, pasta, couscous and bulgur (from wheat), potatoes, polenta (from corn), nuts and seeds.
2. The leading source of fat in the diet is olive oil and is used as the primary cooking oil. It is used in abundance, and approximately 35% of the calories are because of the fats. The critical thing to understand is that saturated fats are only credited with 8% of the total calories, and is even lesser than this in some cases, which means that the consumption of dairy products and meat is limited.
3. Veggies and fruits intake is high in number. Both vegetables and fruits are unprocessed, locally produced, fresh, and eaten in season.
4. Dairy intake is limited in the Mediterranean diet plan. Dairy is consumed mostly in the form of yogurt and cheese with their amounts being 1 cup of yogurt and 1 oz. of cheese.
5. Eggs are consumed in the amount of around four eggs per week.
6. Poultry and fish are allowed only one to three times a week. This means that it should be lower than 1 lb. per week collectively, and fish should be preferred over poultry.

7. Red meat is also consumed in a limited amount, i.e. once in a month, while its quantity should be less than a pound in a single month.
8. Honey is the primary sweetening source in the Mediterranean diet. Sweet intake is also limited in this diet plan and is allowed for consumption a few times every week.
9. Wine intake should be moderate, and i1-2 glasses is allowed every day.

The History of the Mediterranean Diet

The origin of the Mediterranean diet is around the area along the Mediterranean Sea. These areas are also known for the initiators for the origins of the culture of the world. The eating habits of the inhabitants of these areas were developed thousands of years ago. The versatility of dietary habits can be seen in parts of Europe, including Spain, Greece, Southern France, Italy, and Portugal. The Mediterranean diet is also followed in the northern parts of Africa like Tunisia and Morocco. The Mediterranean diet is also followed by the Middle Eastern countries. like Syria and Lebanon. as well as by Balkan states and Turkey. The diet is very popular because the region produces fresh veggies and fruits around the year and is consumed by people frequently. The main produce of the area includes nuts, olive oil, legumes, bread, wine, and an abundant supply of fish from the Mediterranean Sea itself. Meal prepping and sharing it with others is a cultural root of the Mediterranean region, and the cuisine is widespread across the globe for its rich and delicious taste and flavor.

The Science behind the Mediterranean Diet

The Mediterranean diet is based upon the culture and cuisines of the Mediterranean region. Numerous scientific and medical studies have argued and proven that the Mediterranean diet is very healthy and is a perfect diet plan for avoiding various chronic diseases like cancer and cardiac complications. Best of all it boosts life expectancy!

In the 1950s, the medical researchers had started drawing connections between diet and cardiac complications. Dr. Ancel Keys performed a study on various diets in accordance with the principles of epidemiology. The study is known as "Seven Countries Study" and has been declared the most authentic epidemiological study ever conducted. The study involved around 13,000 male individuals from the US, Japan, Serbia, Finland, the Netherlands, and Croatia and was performed over a decade. The study was concluded on the fact that the people from the Mediterranean region had a smaller risk of getting a chronic disease related to the heart and enjoyed more healthy lifestyles as compared to the rest of the world. The study showed that the mortality rate of the Mediterranean region was comparatively low from the rest of the globe too, i.e. Greek men aged 50-54 had 90% lower risk of having a cardiac issue as compared to the same age group from the United States.

The study also showed that the Mediterranean diet is rich in fat content has 40% of its calories subjected to its high fat. The Mediterranean diet is very different in its fat intake from the rest of the diets. Mediterranean cuisine involves a higher content of unsaturated fat like olive oil and a lower content of saturated fats. Saturated fats are mainly present in dairy products and meat, apart from their slight presence in a few nuts, avocados and certain vegetable oils. The saturated fats are utilized by the body to make cholesterol, and it has been proven various times that cardiovascular issues are strongly linked with higher cholesterol levels.

Various scientific research has further backed the work of Dr. Ancle Keys about the healthy lifestyle of the Mediterranean people. An analysis issued by the WHO in 1990 reported that Europe Mediterranean countries, such as Italy, Greece, France, and Spain have a lower risk of heart complications, higher life expectancy, and lower risk of cancer from the rest of Europe. The analysis proved critical as these countries have high smoking populations and are not having any properly conducted exercise programs like the American society. This indicates that this healthy lifestyle has some other factors involved. The element of genetic variations has also been discarded by scientists because Mediterraneans who move to other countries and get off the Mediterranean diet lose the health advantages the diet offered. These studies all confirm the fact that both lifestyle and diet are critically important factors. In 1994, French research indicated that people following the Mediterranean diet are less prone to have cardiac diseases and deaths as compared to other diet followers.

The Mediterranean diet came into the limelight when the head of the Nutrition Department of Harvard University, Dr. Walter Willet, recommended it to various people. Low-fat oriented diets were already being prescribed for heart issues. Mediterranean groups involved in his studies had a high-fat oriented diet, which has its main fat content from olive oil. His studies showed that the risk of heart-related complications and diseases can be lowered by increasing the intake of a type of dietary fat, i.e. the mono-saturated fat, which is present mostly in olive oils. This argument of Dr. Walter was in opposition to the generally applied nutritional preferences and

recommendations of eliminating all kinds of fat content from diet plans to avoid heart-related problems. Researchers have concluded that unsaturated fats have been credited with a high amount of HDL cholesterol, which is also referred to as "the good" cholesterol. The reason for HDL cholesterol being credited as a friend for the body is that it protects the body from cardiovascular complications. Dr. Willet also drew the links between meat intake with cancer and cardiovascular diseases.

Dr. Willet and the WHO, along with various other researchers, joined hands in 1994 and constructed the Mediterranean Food Pyramid. The Mediterranean Food Pyramid involves food from multiple categories and its intake amount per day to perfectly follow the Mediterranean diet plan. These researchers argue that their food groups are far more beneficial in health status as compared to the food groups designed by the United States Department of Agriculture (USDA). The USDA has listed a higher content of daily meat and dairy servings. The Mediterranean diet specialists claim that these recommendations are politically motivated and have nothing to do with dietary science at all.

Chapter-2: Living healthier and longer on the Mediterranean Diet

The Incredible Health Benefits of Eating the Mediterranean Way

As explained above, the Mediterranean diet has various health benefits for its followers if it is followed consistently. Some of the most essential ones are as follows:

1. **Preserve Memory**
The Mediterranean diet is proven to be very beneficial in preserving your memory and preventing cognitive declines. The reason is that the Mediterranean diet is high in its healthy fat content, which is extraordinarily helpful for stimulating the human's brain power, as well as avoiding or lowering the risk of cognitive decline and dementia. Research indicates that regularly following the Mediterranean diet will reduce the risk of cognitive decreases by around 40 percent.

2. **Lower Risk of Cardiovascular Complications**
The Mediterranean diet has a positive effect on heart-related risk factors like triglycerides, high BP, and cholesterol. This is why it reduces the risk of having cardiovascular diseases, such as strokes, myocardial infarction (commonly known as heart attack), and coronary heart disease, etc.

3. **Bone Strengthening**
Olive oil is used in abundance in the Mediterranean diet. Olive oil is credited with preserving and increasing bone density by incrementing the maturity and proliferation of the bone cells. The diet patterns of the Mediterranean diet are also credited with avoiding osteoporosis.

4. **Blood Sugar Controlling**
The Mediterranean diet has been proven to control body blood sugar and diabetes. Research has shown that it can also reverse type-2 diabetes. It is also claimed that the Mediterranean diet can improve heart-related risks and blood sugar control in individuals already having it. The Mediterranean diet followers, when observed showed improved blood sugar, improved weight loss, and a lower urge to get medical treatment compared to those having a low-fat diet plan.

5. **Anti-Depression**

The Mediterranean diet has also been credited as an anti-depressant. A study conducted in 2013 showed that those who follow the Mediterranean diet plan has approximately 98.6% reduced risk of prone to depression than those who follow other diet plans.

6. **Prevents Cancer**

The Mediterranean diet has been credited with anticancer properties. A study shows that those who follow the Mediterranean diet has a 13% reduced risk of having terminal cancer than those who do not follow the diet. The various cancers that can be prevented by following the Mediterranean diet include neck cancer, liver cancer, breast cancer, prostate cancer, head cancer, colorectal cancer, and gastric cancer.

A Delicious Path to Weight Loss

In 2015, the United States released information about how the Mediterranean diet plan was effective in providing you with numerous health benefits. The diet plan, as mentioned earlier, is based on having more seafood and fruit, and comparatively lesser dairy than other healthy diet plans.

To have a perfect and healthy lifestyle with the plan, start it with having plant-based foods. Go for a vast variety of vegetables, fruits, nuts, legumes, and whole grains. Afterwards, change your butter to a more healthy fat like olive oil. Choose spices and herbs to replace salt in your foods. Have your poultry and fish twice in a week. Reduce the consumption of red meat to a few times in a month.

To have a perfect and healthier Mediterranean diet, choose a diet that gives you 1200 calories per day. Initiate it with 1 ½ cups of veggies and keep incrementing them. Over a single week, combine a variety of orange, green, and red vegetables that contain all their micronutrients, and also add some protein and fiber sources, along with a few legumes.

Other foods to have daily include 4 ounces of grains (half of them whole-grains), 1 cup of fruit, 3 ounces of protein sources, like eggs, seeds, seafood, nuts, and poultry, 2 ½ cups of non-fat dairy, and a single tablespoon of oil.

These portion sizes can be customized to your requirements depending upon how fast you want your weight reduction process to be. The Mediterranean diet plan is a complete way of life, once you hit your weight goals, increment the portion sizes to maintain it right there.

Chapter-3: Starting the Mediterranean Diet

Planning your Mediterranean Diet

Although you can find many cookbooks and recipe pamphlets for starting a Mediterranean diet, we are going to explain the necessary steps that lead toward the Mediterranean diet. These include:

1. The first step involves eliminating all kinds of oils, margarine, and butter by replacing them with olive oil.
2. Always consume meats with salads and bread.
3. American followers can visit farmer markets or places selling organic produce to obtain fresh vegetables and fruits.
4. Replace meat with legumes, whole grains, and other foods for various meals.
5. Always have cheese or yogurt instead of milk.
6. Various other factors include having workout sessions to eliminate stress.
7. The most substantial meal, i.e. the lunch, should be followed with a short nap, siesta.

Precautions

1. Do not consume wine if you have any health complications.
2. Only use olive oil in abundance when it is the only oil in your food, not as an additional oil.
3. Lower fat intake from dairy products, hydrogenated cooking oils, and other sources.

The Top 10 tips for Success

The Mediterranean diet has been credited with an abundance of health benefits, which can be quickly gained by simple tricks. The following tricks and tips are going to ensure you are following the Mediterranean diet perfectly. These include:

1. **Doubling or Tripling your Veggies**

An increased amount of vegetables is always beneficial for your health. There is numerous research, which proves that any plant-heavy diet plan has far better health benefits than any other diet plan. According to a study, people who consume 7 or above servings of veggies and fruits have a comparatively lower risk of cardiovascular diseases and cancer. As per the findings of another study, 10 or above servings of fruits and vegetables will reduce the risk of strokes and avoid 7.8 million premature deaths.

2. **Start loving legumes**

Legumes are the most abundant protein resource included in the Mediterranean diet, and they are also credited as the perfect dietary fiber resource available. A single cup of navy beans has more dietary fiber than 7 slices of bread (whole-wheat) and more protein than 2 eggs. Eat more of them.

3. **Consume enough Seafood and Fish**

Seafood and fish are high in proteins, vitamin B & D, selenium, and are also supported by a study that shows how consumption of 2 oz. of fish can lower the risk of death by 12 %. You should preferably consume fatty fishes.

4. Start using Olive oil

The first step for a successful Mediterranean diet is to eliminate all kinds of oils, margarine, and butter by replacing it with olive oil. There are beneficial mono-saturated fats in olive oil, which produce HDL cholesterol. HDL cholesterol is credited with preventing heart issues.

5. Use fruits as desserts

Fruits are low in fat, high in fiber and also perfect antioxidants. Consuming whole-fruit can lower the risk of diabetes. For example, pears and apples are credited with reducing the risk of having heart strokes. You can use fruit as desserts or even snack on them between meals.

6. Garnish using Diary

Allowed dairy products for the Mediterranean diet can be used in small amounts for garnishing. Dairy has been credited with a lower risk of heart diseases, diabetes, obesity, and metabolic syndrome.

7. Increase seasonings

The Mediterranean diet is very dependent on herbs and seasonings instead of salt like the American diet. Garlic has nutrients, which lower bad cholesterol, promote healthy immune functioning, and lowers the risk of cancer. Herbs are also antioxidants in nature and can help you avoid various diseases.

8. Limit Meat Consumption

The regular Mediterranean diet does not have a high content of meat apart from those eaten during religious events. Even when meat is used, it is grass-fed and pasture-raised and contains a higher amount of Omega-3 fatty acids and CLA.

9. Eat Pasta

Pasta is made from durum and is less likely to spike-up your blood sugar levels. You can combine pasta and olive oil to slow down absorption.

10. Socialize your Eating habits

There is no concept of fast food in the Mediterranean diet, so you do not have to eat alone. Instead, eat with your family and loved ones to experience a better taste of food and a healthier life.

Chapter-4 Eating on the Mediterranean Diet

What's on your Plate?

The Mediterranean diet has vast, delicious food options for its followers. The exact foods for the diet seem to be controversial as there is certainly variations among the counties. The foods, which are preferred to be consumed for perfectly following the Mediterranean diet include:

1. **Veggies** like, kale, carrots, broccoli, tomatoes, cauliflower, Brussels sprouts, spinach, cucumbers, etc.
2. **Fruits** like oranges, strawberries, figs, peaches, melons, pears, apples, dates, bananas, grapes, etc.
3. **Seeds and nuts** like macadamia nuts, cashews, pumpkin seeds, almonds, walnuts, hazelnuts, sunflower seeds, etc.
4. **Legumes** like lentils, chickpeas, beans, pulses, peas, peanuts, etc.
5. **Tubers** like yams, sweet potatoes, turnips, potatoes, etc.
6. **Poultry** like turkey, chicken, duck, etc.
7. **Dairy products** like Greek yogurt, cheese, yogurt, etc.
8. **Eggs** like quail eggs, duck eggs, and chicken eggs, etc.
9. **Spices and Herbs** like basil, rosemary, nutmeg, pepper, mint, garlic, sage, cinnamon, etc.
10. **Healthy fats** like avocado oil, olive oil, olives, and avocados, etc.
11. **Whole grains** like rye, corn, barley, wheat oats, whole wheat, pasta and braid (whole grain), corn, brown rice, etc.
12. **Seafood and Fish** like tuna, trout, shrimp, clams, trout, crabs, sardines, mussels, salmon, etc.

Beverages

- The preferred beverage for the Mediterranean diet is water.
- Apart from this, you can have approximately 1-2 glasses of wine daily. But you should not drink wine if you have any complications related to its intake.
- You can also drink tea and coffee, but it is preferable to avoid high-sugar drinks, sugar-sweetened beverages, and various fruit juices.

The essential factors regarding food that should be kept in mind while following the Mediterranean diet are :

- Rarely eat red meat.
- Moderately eat dairy products and poultry.
- You can eat the rest of the foods in abundance.

The No Go

As stated earlier, the Mediterranean diet has vast, delicious food options for its followers, but there is are certain limitations to it too. The foods that should be avoided for perfectly following the Mediterranean diet include

1. **Added sugars** like soda, ice cream, soda, table sugar, and various other same products, etc.
2. **Refined grains** like past (having refined wheat), white bread, etc.
3. **Trans Fats** are containing foods like margarine and other processed foods.
4. **Refined oils** like cottonseed oil, canola oil, soybean oil, etc.
5. **Processed meats** like hot dogs, processed sausages, etc.
6. **Highly processed foods**, i.e. anything labeled "low-fat" or "diet," which indicates that they have been manufactured in a factory.

Your Mediterranean Shopping Diet

It is always recommended to shop for your Mediterranean diet plan at the perimeter of the grocery store. The reason for this is that most of the whole foods are there. Your first priority should always be foods that are the least or not at all processed. Preferably, choose organic foods, if they are affordable for you. A general guidance for shopping is as follows:

- **Veggies:** garlic, spinach, broccoli, carrots, kale, onions, etc.
- **Fruits:** grapes, bananas, apples, oranges, etc.
- **Berries:** blueberries, strawberries, etc.
- **Grains:** whole-grain pasta, whole-grain bread, etc.
- **Frozen veggies:** go for mixes with healthy veggies.
- **Nuts:** cashews, almonds, and nuts, etc.
- **Legumes:** beans, pulses, lentils, etc.
- Chicken
- Olives
- Potatoes
- Greek yogurt
- Shellfish and shrimp
- Sweet potatoes and potatoes
- **Fish:** trout, sardines, salmon, mackerel
- **Condiments:** cinnamon, pepper, salt, turmeric, etc.
- **Seeds:** pumpkin seeds, sunflower seeds, etc.
- Extra virgin olive oil.
- Eggs (omega-3 enriched or pastured)
- Cheese.

Eating Out on the Mediterranean diet

Fast food

The allowed fast foods on the Mediterranean diet includes, salads, veggies, gyros with pita bread, and souvlaki. If you cannot find them, you can still go for a Mediterranean diet fast food by careful selection of foods. You can grab a Pesto/Basil Turkey Frescheta sandwich at Wendy's. The olive oil will not be present in it but eating once in a week or month will not do any harm. The following fast foods are one to say no to on the Mediterranean diet:

- No mayonnaise or chicken spread
- No breaded fried meat or fried potatoes
- No chips, desserts, and soda pops.

Instead choose the following:

- Grilled chicken sandwich with no cheese
- Meal-sized salads having turkeys or chicken

Sandwiches

Choose the low-fat subs available at Subway, even though it will not contain a lot of olive oil. You can also have a chicken spinach or turkey wrap. Avoiding the previously mentioned food to say no to will keep you on the right track.

Pizza

Although Italian pizza is classified as a quintessential Mediterranean food, the American pizza contains high-fat meats and loads of cheese. Go for a thin-crest pizza with no oil on the bottom. Go light on cheese with no meat and veggie toppings. Prefer feta cheese, if you can get any.

High End Eateries

If you can afford a fancy restaurant, where the chefs can make the food that consists of your preferred choices, you are going to be closer to a Mediterranean diet. You are going to find food that was cooked in olive oil most of the times in these restaurants.

Seven-Day Sample Meal Plan

It is necessary to make a meal plan if you are beginning the Mediterranean diet. This meal plan will help you lose weight if you follow it properly. Normally, the length of the week plans varies according to different diets. However, for the followers of the Mediterranean diet, we will provide a seven-day sample meal plan. This is a meal plan along with the delicious and mouthwatering recipes listed below, which can also be extended to a 14-day meal plan or 21- day meal plan. These recipes are tasty and easy to cook for the beginners and followers of the Mediterranean diet. The Seven Days Meal Plan for the Mediterranean Diet is as follows with the breakfast, lunch, and dinner.

For Day 1
Breakfast: Mediterranean Smoothie
Lunch: Spinach Beans
Dinner: Mediterranean Chicken and Orzo
Snacks: Stuffed Tomatoes
Dessert: Honey Yogurt Cheesecake

For Day 2
Breakfast: Soufflé Omelet with Mushrooms
Lunch: Griddled Vegetables and Feta Tart
Dinner: Mediterranean Beef Pinwheels
Snacks: Niçoise toasts
Dessert: Greek Baklava

For Day 3
Breakfast: Spinach Parmesan Baked Eggs
Lunch: Moroccan Couscous
Dinner: Crusty Grilled Mussels
Snacks: Spiced Tortilla
Dessert: Almond Orange Pandoro

For Day 4
Breakfast: Sweet Potato Breakfast Hash
Lunch: Roasted Vegetable Tabbouleh
Dinner: Garlic and Rosemary Mediterranean Pork Roast
Snacks: Ditalini Minestrone
Dessert: Honey Glazed Pears

For Day 5
Breakfast: Green Poached Egg Toasts
Lunch: Bean Mash with Grilled Veggies
Dinner: Hasselback Caprese Chicken
Snacks: Herbed Olives
Dessert: Popped Quinoa Bars

For Day 6
Breakfast: Spinach and Feta Baked Eggs
Lunch: Charred Green Beans with Mustard
Dinner: Saffron Fish Gratins
Snacks: Crispy Squid with Capers
Dessert: Orange Sesame Cookies

For Day 7
Breakfast: Red Smoothie
Lunch: Baked Mediterranean Rice
Dinner: Baked Lamb Tray
Snacks: Crustless Vegetable Quiche
Dessert: Compote Dipped Berries Mix

Breakfast Recipes

Pina Colada Smoothie

Serves: 2
Prep Time: 10 mins
Pina colada is everyone's personal favorite, and is this Pina colada smoothie.

Ingredients
- 1 cup pineapple, peeled and sliced
- 2 bananas
- 1 cup mango, cored and diced
- ½ cup ice
- 2/3 cup coconut milk
- 2 tablespoons flaxseed

Directions
1. Put all the ingredients in a blender and blend until smooth.
2. Pour into 2 glasses and serve immediately.

Nutrition
Calories: 417
Carbs: 56.6g
Fats: 22.1g
Proteins: 5.5g
Sodium: 19mg
Sugar: 36.6g

Green Poached Egg Toasts

Serves: 2
Prep Time: 15 mins
Enjoy the same old morning egg with crispy toast in a more tempting style!

Ingredients
- 2 oz avocado flesh, mashed
- 2 bread slices, toasted
- ¼ teaspoon lemon juice
- 3.5 oz smoked salmon
- 1 teaspoon soy sauce
- 2 eggs

- Salt and black pepper, to taste

Directions
1. Boil water and create a whirlpool in it.
2. Crack an egg in it and allow it to cook.
3. Repeat the same process with the other egg.
4. Transfer both the eggs immediately to an ice bath for 10 seconds.
5. Scoop out the fresh avocado flesh into a bowl and mash well.
6. Place 2 toasted slices in the serving plates and spread the avocado mash generously over them.
7. Divide the smoked salmon over the bread slices.
8. Drizzle half of the soy sauce, lemon juice, salt and black pepper over each of the toasts.
9. Top each with one poached egg and serve.

Nutrition
Calories: 195
Carbs: 7.8g
Fats: 11.2g
Proteins: 16.1g
Sodium: 1267mg
Sugar: 1g

Kiwi Smoothie

Serves: 1
Prep Time: 10 mins
Add this delicious fruit to your diet and make a refreshing smoothie out of it.

Ingredients
- ½ cup fresh pineapple
- ½ cup basil leaves
- 5 kiwis
- 1 banana

Directions
1. Put all the ingredients in a blender and blend until smooth.
2. Pour into a glass and immediately serve.

Nutrition
Calories: 378
Carbs: 93.5g
Fats: 2.5g
Proteins: 6.1g
Sodium: 14mg
Sugar: 56.7g

Soufflé Omelet with Mushrooms

Serves: 6
Prep Time: 25 mins
This soufflé omelet has this soft and spongy texture, which can get your morning to a good start.

Ingredients
- 1 garlic clove, minced
- 1 tablespoon parsley, minced
- ½ teaspoon salt
- ¼ cup cheddar cheese, grated
- 1 teaspoon extra-virgin olive oil
- 8 ounces sliced mushrooms
- 3 large eggs, separated
- ½ teaspoon black pepper

Directions
1. Heat oil in a nonstick skillet over medium-high heat and add garlic.
2. Sauté for 1 minute and stir in the mushrooms.
3. Cook for about 10 minutes and drizzle parsley on top.
4. Beat egg yolks in a bowl and whisk the egg whites separately.
5. Season this mixture with salt, black pepper, and cheese.
6. Warm a large skillet on medium heat and pour in the egg batter.
7. Cover the lid and spread mushroom over one side of the egg.
8. Fold it over the mushrooms and dish out to serve.

Nutrition
Calories: 142
Carbs: 3.6g
Fats: 9.9g
Proteins: 11.2g
Sodium: 521mg
Sugar: 1.8g

Spinach Parmesan Baked Eggs

Serves: 4
Prep Time: 25 mins
Try a unique combination of baked eggs with parmesan and spinach!

Ingredients
- 2 cloves garlic, minced
- ½ cup fat-free parmesan cheese, grated
- 1 small tomato, diced small
- 2 teaspoons olive oil
- 4 cups baby spinach
- 4 eggs

Directions
1. Preheat the oven to 350 degrees F and grease an 8-inch casserole dish.
2. Heat olive oil in a large skillet over medium heat and stir in garlic and spinach.
3. Sauté until spinach is wilted and drain completely.
4. Add parmesan cheese and transfer this mixture to the casserole dish.
5. Make four wells in the spinach mixture and crack one egg into each well.
6. Place the casserole dish in the oven and bake for about 15 minutes.
7. Dish out and serve warm.

Nutrition
Calories: 231
Carbs: 4.3g
Fats: 15.9g
Proteins: 20.2g
Sodium: 477mg
Sugar: 1.1g

Red smoothie

Serves: 1
Prep Time: 10 mins
The name red smoothie comes from the color of the raspberry and flavored with lemon juice.

Ingredients
- 3 tablespoons raspberry
- 4 plums, cored
- 3 tablespoons blueberry
- 1 teaspoon linseed oil
- 1 tablespoon lemon juice

Directions
1. Put all the ingredients in a blender and blend until smooth.
2. Pour into a glass and immediately serve.

Nutrition
Calories: 151
Carbs: 39g
Fats: 1.2g
Proteins: 2.6g
Sodium: 3mg
Sugar: 32g

Sweet Potato Breakfast Hash

Serves: 6
Prep Time: 30 mins
Sweet potatoes when cooked with a mixture of ham and avocado will melt your heart away.

Ingredients
- 3 tablespoons olive oil
- ¼ teaspoon ground white pepper
- 2 cloves garlic, minced
- 2 sweet potatoes, peeled and cubed
- ½ teaspoon salt
- 1 tablespoon apple cider vinegar
- 1 teaspoon honey
- ¼ cup yellow onion, diced
- 8 ounces low sodium sulfate free ham, diced
- 1 tablespoon lemon juice
- ¼ cup green bell pepper, diced
- 1 avocado, peeled, pit removed, and diced

Directions
1. Preheat the oven to 450 degrees F and grease a baking sheet.
2. Season the sweet potatoes with black pepper and salt, and drizzle with a half tablespoon olive oil.
3. Arrange these seasoned potatoes in the baking sheet and transfer in the oven.
4. Bake for about 15 minutes and remove from the oven.
5. Combine apple cider vinegar, 1 tablespoon olive oil, garlic, and honey in a small bowl.
6. Heat the skillet and add remaining olive oil in it.
7. Stir in bell pepper and onion and sauté until soft.
8. Add baked potatoes and ham and cook until the meat turns golden.
9. Turn off the heat and season the mixture with vinegar sauce, lemon juice, and avocado.
10. Dish out and serve warm.

Nutrition
Calories: 382 Carbs: 23.4g Fats: 23.4g Proteins: 20.4g Sodium: 1679mg Sugar: 1.9g

Spinach and Feta Baked Egg

Serves: 4
Prep Time: 25 mins
These spinach-lined eggs muffin cups are simple to cook yet richer and healthier in content.

Ingredients
- 4 eggs
- 1 cup cooked spinach, squeezed
- ½ cup fat-free feta cheese

Directions
1. Preheat the oven to 370 degrees F and grease a muffin pan with muffin cups.
2. Divide the spinach into four muffin cups and press gently into the bottom.
3. Stir in whisked eggs and top with feta cheese.
4. Bake for about 15 minutes and dish out to serve warm.

Nutrition
Calories: 114
Carbs: 1.4g
Fats: 8.4g
Proteins: 8.4g
Sodium: 277mg
Sugar: 1.1g

Mediterranean Smoothie

Serves: 1
Prep Time: 10 mins
This smoothie is the mother of all smoothies as it contains all the right ingredients to make it a super Mediterranean drink.

Ingredients
- 1 teaspoon fresh ginger root, minced
- 2 cups baby spinach, loosely packed
- 1 frozen banana
- ½ cup beet juice
- 6 ice cubes
- 1 small mango
- ½ cup coconut milk

Directions
1. Put all the ingredients in a blender and blend until smooth.
2. Pour into a glass and serve immediately.

Nutrition
Calories: 528
Carbs: 125.5g
Fats: 1.7g
Proteins: 13.1g
Sodium: 432mg
Sugar: 84.9g

Small Plates and Snacks Recipes

Niçoise toasts

Serves: 4
Prep Time: 20 mins
These toasts have all the ingredients which can guarantee good taste and lots of nutrients.

Ingredients
- 3 tablespoons olive oil
- 2 garlic cloves, crushed
- 1½ cups tomatoes, chopped

- 2 tablespoons mini capers, drained
- 12 pitted black olives, drained and halved
- Baby basil leaves, to serve
- 1 (¾ cup) part-baked baguette, cut into 24 circles
- 6 anchovy fillets in olive oil, drained
- ½ medium red onion, finely chopped
- 2 tablespoons tomato purée
- ½ teaspoon chili flakes
- 2 tablespoons parmesan, finely grated

Directions
1. Preheat the oven to 375 degrees F and grease a baking sheet.
2. Arrange the bread slices on the baking sheet and drizzle with a tablespoon of olive oil.
3. Bake for about 12 minutes and keep aside.
4. Heat the rest of the oil in a nonstick skillet and add onion, garlic, and anchovies.
5. Sauté for about 4 minutes and add puree, tomatoes, caper, and chili flakes.
6. Cook this mixture with occasional stirring and spoon out this mixture over the baked slices.
7. Divide half of the olives over each piece and top with parmesan cheese.
8. Cover the slices and refrigerate overnight.
9. Place the pizza toasts in the oven and bake for about 8 minutes.
10. Serve garnished with basil leaves and enjoy.

Nutrition
Calories: 328
Carbs: 19.8g
Fats: 23g
Proteins: 14.1g
Sodium: 2154mg
Sugar: 3.6g

Herbed Olives

Serves: 6
Prep Time: 5 mins
Serve these yummy herbed olives as a side meal and also as the snack.

Ingredients
- 2 teaspoons extra-virgin olive oil
- ⅛ teaspoon dried basil
- Black pepper, to taste
- 3 cups olives
- ⅛ teaspoon dried oregano
- 1 garlic clove, crushed

Directions
1. Toss the olives with all other ingredients in a bowl.
2. Insert a toothpick into each olive and serve.

Nutrition
Calories: 93
Carbs: 4.7g
Fats: 8.8g
Proteins: 0.7g
Sodium: 586mg
Sugar: 0g

Stuffed tomatoes

Serves: 6
Prep Time: 30 mins
These stuffed tomatoes are a healthy side meal for all the festive dinners.

Ingredients
- 2 mozzarella balls, sliced
- 6 large tomatoes, heads chopped and seeds removed
- 12 basil leaves, fresh
- 2 tablespoons red pesto
- 4 pieces red peppers, cooked

Directions
1. Preheat the oven to 375 degrees F and grease a baking sheet.
2. Arrange the tomatoes on a baking sheet with their cut side up.
3. Top the tomato bases with chopped mozzarella cheese, red peppers, and basil leaves.
4. Repeat the layers and top each base with a dollop of pesto.
5. Cover the tomato bases with their chopped off heads.
6. Transfer into the oven and bake for about 20 minutes.
7. Dish out and serve immediately.

Nutrition
Calories: 280
Carbs: 30.9g
Fats: 14.6g
Proteins: 8.5g
Sodium: 248mg
Sugar: 6.7g

Crispy Squid with Capers

Serves: 6
Prep Time: 25 mins
Along with the squids, the capers are also coated and deep fried to make a tempting delight.

Ingredients
- 7 oz. whole wheat flour
- 1 garlic clove, crushed
- 10 oz. baby squid, cleaned and sliced into thick rings
- 2 tablespoons caper, drained and finely chopped
- 5 tablespoons mayonnaise
- Lemon wedges, to serve
- Vegetable oil, for frying

Directions
1. Mix together squid, capers and whole wheat flour in a shallow bowl.
2. Heat oil in a wok and deep fry capers and squids.
3. When fried to a golden color, dish out the capers and squid in a plate.
4. Serve with garlic, mayonnaise, and lemon wedges.

Nutrition
Calories: 213
Carbs: 29.9g
Fats: 5.1g
Proteins: 11g
Sodium: 194mg
Sugar: 0.9g

Spiced Tortilla

Serves: 4
Prep Time: 25 mins
This spiced tortilla is made out of eggs, unlike the flour tortilla.

Ingredients
- 1 onion, sliced
- 2 teaspoons curry spice
- 1 pound cooked potatoes, sliced
- 8 eggs, beaten
- 1 tablespoon sunflower oil
- 1 red chili, deseeded and shredded
- 1½ cups cherry tomatoes
- 1 bunch coriander, finely chopped

Directions
1. Heat oil in a skillet and add half of the chili and onion.
2. Sauté for about 5 minutes and add the spices, potatoes, coriander stalks, and tomatoes.
3. Whisk the eggs with seasoning and pour it into the pan.
4. Cook for about 10 minutes until it is set.
5. Preheat the grill and transfer the pan into the grill.
6. Grill for about 2 minutes and garnish with the remaining chilies and coriander leaves.
7. Slice and serve to enjoy.

Nutrition
Calories: 261
Carbs: 24.3g
Fats: 12.5g
Proteins: 14.1g
Sodium: 135mg
Sugar: 2.8g

Crustless Vegetable Quiche

Serves: 4
Prep Time: 40 mins
The crustless vegetable quiche, having the distinct flavors of the dried herbs, will become the ultimate love for veggies lovers.

Ingredients
- 1 small yellow onion, diced
- ½ cup red bell pepper, diced
- ½ cup zucchini, sliced
- 1 tablespoon olive oil
- 2 garlic cloves, minced
- ½ cup green bell pepper, diced
- 6 broccoli florets
- 3 large eggs
- 2 tablespoons coconut milk
- ½ teaspoon black pepper
- ¼ cup low-fat parmesan cheese
- ¼ cup sun-dried tomatoes, diced
- 4 large egg whites
- 1 teaspoon dried oregano
- Sea salt, to taste

Directions
1. Preheat the oven to 425 degrees F and grease a 9-inch pie dish.
2. Heat oil in a large skillet over medium heat and add onion and garlic.
3. Sauté for about 4 minutes and add zucchini, broccoli, bell pepper, and dried tomatoes.
4. Sauté for about 2 minutes and dish out in a bowl.
5. Whisk eggs with spices, milk, egg whites, and ¼ cup parmesan cheese.
6. Stir in sautéed egg mixture and transfer the batter into a pie dish.
7. Place in the oven and bake for about 10 minutes.
8. Reduce the heat to 350 degrees F and bake for about 20 minutes.
9. Top with parmesan cheese and serve.

Nutrition
Calories: 180 Carbs: 10.4g Fats: 9.9g Proteins: 14.5g Sodium: 222mg Sugar: 4.2g

Ditalini Minestrone

Serves: 4
Prep Time: 30 mins

This Ditalini Minestrone is made with a combination of vegetables, which are cooked in hot
stock along with beans and pasta.

Ingredients
- 1 onion, chopped
- 2 celery stalks, chopped
- 1 teaspoon salt
- 2 cups water
- ½ cup tomato sauce
- ¼ cup olive oil
- 2 carrots, chopped
- 3 garlic cloves, minced
- ¼ teaspoon black pepper
- 4 cups chicken stock
- 3 sprigs fresh thyme
- 2 cups swiss chard, chopped
- 1 can cannellini beans
- 1 pinch red pepper flakes
- Olive oil, to drizzle
- 1 bay leaf
- 1 cup Napa cabbage, chopped
- ⅔ cup ditalini pasta
- Parmesan cheese ribbons, for garnish

Directions
1. Heat olive oil in a cooking pot and add celery, onions, and carrots.
2. Sauté until soft and stir in salt, black pepper, and garlic.
3. Cook for about 1 minute and pour in the stock, water, tomato sauce, thyme, and bay leaf.
4. Boil the soup and add spinach, red pepper flakes, and cabbage.
5. Cook until the veggies turn soft and add pasta.
6. Cook until al dente and garnish with lemon juice, parmesan cheese, and olive oil.
7. Dish out and serve immediately.

Nutrition
Calories: 346 Carbs: 44.6g Fats: 13.9g Proteins: 14.6g Sodium: 1573mg Sugar: 6.5g

Baked Kale and Eggs with Ricotta

Serves: 4
Prep Time: 30 mins
Kale turns more nutritious than ever when added to an egg recipe and is excellent to have
to start off a good morning.

Ingredients
- 1 tablespoon olive oil
- ¼ cup ricotta cheese, fat-free
- 6 cups kale, stems removed and chopped
- 2 garlic cloves, chopped
- ¼ cup fat-free feta cheese, crumbled
- 1/3 cup grape tomatoes, cut in half
- ½ teaspoon salt
- 4 large eggs
- ¼ teaspoon black pepper

Directions
1. Preheat the oven to 350 degrees F and grease a casserole dish.
2. Heat a skillet on medium heat and stir in garlic and kale.
3. Sauté for about 30 seconds and transfer garlic mixture to a bowl.
4. Mix feta cheese and ricotta cheese in another bowl.
5. Spread the kale mixture in the casserole dish and make about 4 wells in the kale mixture.
6. Crack one egg into each well and spread cheese mixture spoon by spoon on top.
7. Top with tomatoes and sprinkle with salt and black pepper.
8. Bake for about 20 minutes until golden brown and dish out to serve hot.

Nutrition
Calories: 202 Carbs: 13.2g Fats: 11.7g Proteins: 12.6g Sodium: 529mg Sugar: 1.2g

Ham and Poached Egg English Muffin

Serves: 4
Prep Time: 10 mins
Top the English muffins with ham, tomato, and a poached egg to make an ultra-Mediterranean snack.

Ingredients
- 3 teaspoons olive oil
- 2 whole wheat English muffins, halved
- Black pepper, to taste
- 1 tomato, quartered
- 4 ham slices
- 4 eggs, poached

Directions
1. Heat 2 teaspoons of olive oil in a skillet and add ham and tomatoes.
2. Sauté until the meat turns golden and place the ham over the English muffin and tomatoes.
3. Top these muffins with poached eggs and drizzle with olive oil.
4. Season with black pepper and serve.

Nutrition
Calories: 257
Carbs: 16.9g
Fats: 19.4g
Proteins: 6.5g
Sodium: 294mg
Sugar: 2.7g

Salads and Soups Recipes

Red Barley Soup

Serves: 4
Prep Time: 1 hour 10 mins
Barley is a basic ingredient of this soup, which makes it highly nutritious.

Ingredients
- ½ cup barley
- 2 small onions, diced
- 1 celery stalk
- 2 bay leaves
- 7 cups water
- 1 teaspoon salt
- 3 tablespoons red wine
- Brown bread cubes, to serve

- ½ pound small red lentils, dried
- ½ cup olive oil
- 2 medium carrots, diced
- 6 garlic cloves
- 1½ cups tomato sauce
- 2 teaspoons smoked paprika
- 1 tablespoon dried Greek oregano
- Black pepper, to taste
- Cheddar cheese, to serve

Directions
1. Put the lentils and water in a cooking pot and boil for 5 minutes.
2. Stir in barley along with all the other ingredients and 6 cups of water.
3. Cover and cook for about 45 minutes until it thickens.
4. Remove the bay leaves and garnish with cheddar cheese to serve.

Nutrition
Calories: 470
Carbs: 51.5g
Fats: 26.9g
Proteins: 11.8g
Sodium: 2391mg
Sugar: 18g

Mediterranean Sardine Salad

Serves: 4
Prep Time: 20 mins
Sardines are a great seafood, and it tastes amazing when tossed in a refreshing salad.

Ingredients
- ½ cup black olives, roughly chopped
- 2 (7 oz.) cans sardines in tomato sauce
- 1 tablespoon red wine vinegar
- 3 oz. salad leaves
- 1 tablespoon caper, drained and diced
- 1 tablespoon olive oil

Directions
1. Divide the salad leaves into 4 plates and top with capers and olives.
2. Drain the sardines and reserve the sauce.

3. Roughly slice the sardines and divide it between the plates.
4. Drizzle with olive oil, vinegar and tomato sauce to serve.

Nutrition
Calories: 249
Carbs: 5.7g
Fats: 17.1g
Proteins: 16.6g
Sodium: 619mg
Sugar: 2.1g

Greek Meatball Soup

Serves: 4
Prep Time: 40 mins
This Greek meatball soup is a special delicacy of the Mediterranean states, loved because of the unique lemon-egg mixture.

Ingredients
For the Meatballs
- ½ cup medium grain rice
- 1 pound lean ground beef
- 1 small onion, grated
- 3 tablespoons fresh dill, minced
- 1½ teaspoons salt
- 2 tablespoons olive oil
- ½ cup whole wheat flour
- ½ cup fresh parsley, minced
- ½ teaspoon black pepper
- 2 tablespoons water

For the egg-lemon broth
- 2 egg yolks
- 1 whole egg
- 4 tablespoons lemon juice
- 2 teaspoons cornstarch

Directions
1. Stir the meat with rice, salt, dill, parsley, water, olive oil, black pepper, and onion in a large bowl.
2. Cover this meat mixture and refrigerate for about 15 minutes.
3. Make 30 meatballs of golf balls size out of this mixture.
4. Prepare the soup by boiling 8 cups water in a large soup pot.

5. Add ½ teaspoon salt and 3 tablespoons olive oil.
6. Place the meatballs in this soup and cover it partially.
7. Cook the soup for 30 mins approximately, on a simmer.
8. Beat egg with egg yolks in a suitable bowl until frothy.
9. Mix cornstarch with lemon juice, and pour this slurry into the soup.
10. Once the soup turns creamy, stir in the egg mixture.
11. Garnish with olive oil and parsley to serve.

Nutrition
Calories: 480 Carbs: 35.1g Fats: 17.9g Proteins: 42.6g Sodium: 131mg Sugar: 1.3g

Aubergine and Pepper Salad

Serves: 8
Prep Time: 40 mins
This salad is made out of grilled aubergine and roasted peppers that are baked with garlic to get the aromatic flavors.

Ingredients
- 3 aubergines
- 1¼ cups ready-roasted red pepper, soaked and drained
- 2 tablespoons olive oil
- ¼ cup thyme leaves
- 2 garlic cloves, sliced

Directions
1. Preheat the oven to 325 degrees F and grease a baking tray.
2. Set the griddle pan over high heat and add oil and aubergines.
3. Cook for about 3 minutes per side until grilled.
4. Add the grilled aubergines and red peppers to a baking tray.
5. Drizzle with olive oil and top with thyme leaves, seasoning and garlic slices.
6. Transfer the baking tray in the oven and bake for about 30 minutes.
7. Dish out to serve immediately.

Nutrition
Calories: 211
Carbs: 43.2g
Fats: 1g
Proteins: 7.6g
Sodium: 571mg
Sugar: 16.5g

Zucchini Soup

Serves: 6
Prep Time: 30 mins
This mouthwatering zucchini soup is famous for its ultimate richness.

Ingredients
- 8 oz. baby Bella mushrooms, sliced
- 1 bunch flat leaf parsley, chopped
- 2 celery ribs, chopped
- 2 golden potatoes, peeled and diced
- 1 teaspoon ground coriander
- ½ teaspoon thyme
- 1 (32 oz.) can whole peeled tomatoes
- 6 cups turkey bone broth
- 1 lime zest
- 1/3 cup pine nuts, toasted
- 2 tablespoons olive oil
- 2 medium-sized zucchinis, sliced
- 1 medium-sized yellow onion, chopped
- 2 garlic cloves, chopped
- 2 carrots, peeled and chopped
- ½ teaspoon turmeric powder
- ½ teaspoon sweet paprika
- Salt and black pepper, to taste
- 2 bay leaves
- 1 (15 oz.) can chickpeas, rinsed and drained
- 1 lime, juiced

Directions
1. Preheat 1 tablespoon olive oil in an iron cooking pot on medium heat.
2. Stir in mushrooms and sauté for about 4 minutes.
3. Transfer the mushrooms into a flat plate and keep aside.
4. Toss the sliced zucchini into the pot and sauté for about 5 minutes.
5. Dish out the sautéed zucchini into a plate.
6. Heat more oil in that same pan and add celery, potatoes, garlic, and onion.
7. Cook these veggies for about 7 minutes and season the mixture with pepper, salt, and other spices.
8. Stir in bay leaves, tomatoes and broth and bring to a boil.
9. Cover the soup with a lid and allow it to simmer for about 5 minutes.
10. Uncover the soup and add chickpeas, sautéed mushrooms, and zucchini.
11. Let the soup cook for 5 more minutes and garnish with pine nuts to serve.

Nutrition
Calories: 470
Carbs: 78.9g
Fats: 10.2g
Proteins: 22.6g
Sodium: 1040mg
Sugar: 16.7g

Black Beans Feta Salad

Serves: 24
Prep Time: 25 mins
This salad has balanced nutritional values and is an ecstasy for everyone.

Ingredients
- 2 (14.5 ounce) cans black beans, drained
- 4 Roma tomatoes, chopped
- ½ red onion, sliced
- 1 lemon, juiced
- 2 tablespoons olive oil
- Salt, to taste
- ¼ cup fresh dill, chopped
- ¼ cup feta cheese, crumbled

Directions
1. Put all the ingredients in a bowl, except feta and salt.
2. Garnish the beans salad with feta and salt and serve.

Nutrition
Calories: 362
Carbs: 38.2g
Fats: 19.8g
Proteins: 14.1g
Sodium: 265mg
Sugar: 12.8g

Napoletana Hoki Soup

Serves: 4
Prep Time: 30 mins
This soup is a direct source of seafood and several minerals and vitamins.

Ingredients
- 2 cups fish stock
- 1 bulb fennel, finely sliced
- 1 handful basil leaves, torn
- 5 tablespoons half-fat crème Fraiche, to serve
- 1 pound Napoletana pasta sauce
- 2 zucchinis, finely sliced
- 1 pound hoki fillet, defrosted
- 1 teaspoon chipotle chili in adobo sauce or chili paste, to serve

Directions
1. Boil pasta sauce and stock in a large cooking pan.
2. Let it simmer for about 3 minutes and stir in zucchinis and fennel.
3. Cook for about 2 minutes and add the hoki fillets.
4. Cook for about 3 minutes on low heat and add seasoning and basil.
5. Mix crème Fraiche with chili paste and season in a small bowl.
6. Garnish the soup with this seasoned crème Fraiche and serve.

Nutrition
Calories: 459
Carbs: 44.5g
Fats: 21.8g
Proteins: 18.6g
Sodium: 1312mg
Sugar: 7.5g

Chickpeas Pepper Salad

Serves: 2
Prep Time: 30 mins
This chickpeas pepper salad is both good for the lunchtime entrees or the side meal.

Ingredients
- 2 cups water
- ¼ cup red wine vinegar
- 1 red bell pepper, diced
- 4 sun-dried tomatoes
- 2 garlic cloves, chopped
- 2 (14.5 ounce) cans chickpeas, drained and rinsed
- Salt, to taste
- 2 tablespoons extra-virgin olive oil

- ½ cup parsley, chopped

Directions
1. Preheat the oven to 350 degrees F and grease a baking tray.
2. Spread the red bell pepper slices in a baking tray with skin side up.
3. Bake for about 8 minutes and transfer the baked pepper to a ziplock bag.
4. Zip the bag and let it sit for 10 minutes then thinly slice the pepper.
5. Pour 2 cups of water in a bowl and microwave for about 4 minutes.
6. Soak sun-dried tomatoes to the hot water and let it sit for 10 minutes.
7. Drain these tomatoes and slice them thinly.
8. Toss garlic with olive oil and red wine vinegar in a bowl.
9. Add sliced bell pepper, salt, parsley, chickpeas, and sun-dried tomatoes to serve.

Nutrition
Calories: 319 Carbs: 38.3g Fats: 15.8g Proteins: 9.4g Sodium: 251mg Sugar: 15.8g

Passata Cream Soup

Serves: 4
Prep Time: 40 mins
Passata is the special tomato sauce, which enriches this soup. Serve it with breadsticks.

Ingredients
- ½ onion, finely chopped
- 1 celery stick, finely chopped
- 4 large ripe tomatoes
- 2 tablespoons cream
- Shaved parmesan, chopped basil or pesto
- 2 tablespoons olive oil
- 1 small carrot, finely chopped
- ½ cup passata
- ½ vegetable stock
- 4 oz. soup pasta, cooked

Directions
1. Heat oil in a saucepan on low heat and add onion, celery, and carrots.
2. Sauté for about 10 minutes until soft and add the passata sauce and tomatoes.
3. Add water, stock, seasoning and sugar and cook for about 20 minutes.
4. Stir in boiled pasta and cream with gentle stirring.

5. Garnish with parmesan, basil, and pesto to serve.

Nutrition
Calories: 237
Carbs: 35g
Fats: 8.4g
Proteins: 6.2g
Sodium: 178mg
Sugar: 7.7g

Beans, Rice and Grains Recipes

Spinach Beans

Serves: 2
Prep Time: 30 mins
This delightful spinach beans recipe is a perfect luncheon for any day.

Ingredients
- 1 small onion, chopped
- 1 can (14½ ounces) diced tomatoes, undrained
- ¼ teaspoon salt
- 1 can (15 ounces) cannellini beans, rinsed and drained
- 6 ounces fresh baby spinach
- 1 tablespoon olive oil
- 2 garlic cloves, minced
- 2 tablespoons Worcestershire sauce
- ¼ teaspoon black pepper
- 1/8 teaspoon red pepper flakes, crushed
- 14 ounces bacon, chopped

Directions
1. Heat oil in a skillet and add bacon.
2. Sauté until brown and stir in onions.
3. Sauté for about 5 minutes and add garlic to the pan.
4. Cook for about 1 minute and add Worcestershire sauce, seasonings, and tomatoes.
5. Lower the heat and cook for another 8 minutes.
6. Toss in beans and spinach and cook for about 5 minutes.
7. Stir gently and serve immediately.

Nutrition
Calories: 475 Carbs: 77.8g Fats: 8.5g Proteins: 28.2g Sodium: 628mg Sugar: 10.1g

Meatballs Chickpea Medley

Serves: 6
Prep Time: 25 mins
This chickpea medley has all the essential ingredients of a Mediterranean diet with the topping of the meatballs.

Ingredients
- ¼ cup whole wheat panko breadcrumbs
- ¼ cup fresh parsley, chopped
- 1 pound ground chicken
- 2 egg whites
- ¼ cup fat-free feta cheese, crumbled
- 2 tablespoons fresh rosemary, chopped
- 1 tablespoon olive oil
- ½ teaspoon salt
- 1 (15 ounces) can chickpeas, drained
- 3 garlic cloves, roughly chopped
- 1 cup cherry tomatoes

Directions
1. Preheat the oven to 400 degrees F and grease a baking sheet.
2. Whisk egg white in a bowl along with panko, parsley, chicken, feta and rosemary.
3. Toss chickpeas with olive oil, salt, garlic, and tomatoes in a separate bowl.
4. Spread the chickpea mixture on the baking sheet.
5. Use the chicken mince mixture to make 2-inch balls and place these balls over the chickpeas.
6. Bake for about 20 minutes in the oven and immediately serve.

Nutrition
Calories: 473 Carbs: 49.6g Fats: 13.9g Proteins: 38.5g Sodium: 363mg Sugar: 10.5g

Lemony Mushroom and Herb Rice

Serves: 4
Prep Time: 20 mins
Lemony mushroom and herb rice are served with chives and parsley when cooked and fluffed.

Ingredients
- 1¼ cups chestnut mushrooms, diced
- 2 large garlic cloves, finely chopped
- 1 cup long grain rice
- 2 tablespoons olive oil
- 5 tablespoons parsley, chopped
- 1 lemon zest, finely grated
- 3 tablespoons chives, snipped

Directions
1. Boil water with salt in a pan and add rice.
2. Cook for about 10 minutes with constant stirring and drain them through a sieve.
3. Sauté mushrooms for about 4 minutes and stir in garlic.
4. Sauté for about 1 minute and toss in lemon zest, chives, parsley, and drained rice.
5. Serve to enjoy.

Nutrition
Calories: 281
Carbs: 43.6g
Fats: 8.9g
Proteins: 9g
Sodium: 23mg
Sugar: 0.8g

Citrus Garlic Beans

Serves: 2
Prep Time: 25 mins
Citrus Garlic Beans are an anytime, anywhere meal with zesty and juicy butter beans.

Ingredients
- 1 large onion, sliced
- 2 (14 oz.) cans beans, rinsed and drained
- 1 tablespoon olive oil
- 1 garlic clove, crushed
- 1 lemon zest
- 1 large bunch parsley, chopped
- 1 lemon, juiced

Directions
1. Heat oil in a pan and add onions.
2. Sauté for about 3 minutes until soft and stir in the beans and garlic.
3. Cook thoroughly and add lemon zest and lemon juice.
4. Garnish with parsley and serve to enjoy.

Nutrition
Calories: 212
Carbs: 27.5g
Fats: 8.1g
Proteins: 7.9g
Sodium: 533mg
Sugar: 3.2g

Cashew Rice

Serves: 4
Prep Time: 30 mins
Have you ever imagined a fruity rice recipe? This combination has made it all very real with mango sauce.

Ingredients
- 3 cups cooked basmati rice, cooled
- 4 oz. cashew nuts
- 1 green bell pepper, deseeded and finely sliced
- 1 small red onion, finely sliced
- 1 yellow bell pepper, deseeded and finely sliced

For the dressing
- 2 tablespoons light soy sauce
- 1 tablespoon brown sugar
- ½ lemon, juiced
- 3 tablespoons mango chutney

- 1 tablespoon oil
- 2 teaspoons curry powder

Directions
1. Put all the ingredients for dressing in a bowl.
2. Toast the cashews until golden brown and transfer to the mixed dressing.
3. Add rice, onions and bell peppers to serve.

Nutrition
Calories: 433
Carbs: 70.6g
Fats: 17.1g
Proteins: 10.3g
Sodium: 2384mg
Sugar: 14.1g

Moroccan Couscous

Serves: 8
Prep Time: 20 mins
This Moroccan Couscous has a tropical flavor that makes it highly palatable and mouthwatering.

Ingredients
- 1 orange zest
- 1/3 cup dried apricots, chopped
- ¼ teaspoon ground cinnamon
- 1½ cups vegetable stock
- 1 orange, juiced
- 1/3 cup dates, chopped
- 1/3 cup golden raisins
- ½ teaspoon ground cumin
- ½ teaspoon ground ginger
- 2 cups whole-wheat couscous
- ½ cup slivered almonds, toasted
- Salt, to taste
- ¼ teaspoon coriander
- ½ teaspoon turmeric
- 1 tablespoon butter
- ¼ cup mint, chopped

Directions
1. Boil stock in a medium saucepan and add the orange juice, zest, dates, apricots, raisins, couscous, and spices.
2. Remove the pan from the heat and allow the couscous to absorb the liquid for about 15 minutes.
3. Stir in the butter, mint and almonds and season with salt to serve.

Nutrition
Calories: 264 Carbs: 48g Fats: 5g Proteins: 8g Sodium: 124mg Sugar: 13g

Greek Stock Beans

Serves: 2
Prep Time: 35 mins
The slow simmering in this recipe infused strong and deeper flavors into the beans.

Ingredients
- 1 tablespoon red wine vinegar
- 2 tablespoons tomato purée
- 1 large onion, chopped
- 2 cups chicken stock
- 2 (14 oz.) can butter beans, drained
- 1 small bunch dill, chopped
- 2 tablespoons crumbled feta cheese

Directions
1. Heat oil in a skillet on medium heat and add garlic, onions, and seasonings.
2. Sauté for about 8 minutes and add tomato puree, beans, vinegar, stock, and dill.
3. Let it simmer for about 15 minutes and garnish with dill leaves and feta cheese to serve.

Nutrition
Calories: 256
Carbs: 42.7g
Fats: 4.1g
Proteins: 14.2g
Sodium: 900mg
Sugar: 8.6g

Baked Mediterranean Rice

Serves: 8
Prep Time: 50 mins
Have you heard of baked rice? Try this Mediterranean recipe and you will love it.

Ingredients
- 1½ cups arborio rice
- 2 tablespoons fresh oregano, chopped
- 1 pint cherry tomatoes, cut in half
- 2 tablespoons fresh basil, chopped
- ¼ cup Parmesan cheese, grated
- ½ cup sweet onion, diced
- 3 cups chicken broth
- 2 tablespoons butter, melted
- 1 teaspoon salt
- 8 ounces baby spinach, stem tips removed
- ¼ cup fresh parsley, chopped
- 1 cup mozzarella cheese, shredded

Directions
1. Preheat the oven to 370 degrees F and grease a casserole dish.
2. Layer the rice, onions and melted butter into the casserole.
3. Put basil, oregano and salt into the chicken broth and mix well.
4. Pour this mixture over the rice and top evenly with halved tomatoes.
5. Transfer into the oven and bake for about 30 minutes.
6. Remove from the oven and stir in the baby spinach and mozzarella cheese.
7. Top with parsley and grated Parmesan cheese to serve.

Nutrition
Calories: 203 Carbs: 33.2g Fats: 4.7g Proteins: 7g Sodium: 655mg Sugar: 1.9g

Bean Mash with Grilled Veggies

Serves: 2
Prep Time: 20 mins
A bean mash with grilled vegetables is a nice combination if you are not up for a whole bean recipe.

Ingredients

- 1 aubergine, sliced lengthwise
- 2 tablespoons olive oil
- 1 red bell pepper, deseeded and quartered
- 2 zucchinis, sliced lengthwise

For the mash

- 1 garlic clove, crushed
- 1 tablespoon coriander, chopped
- 14 oz. can haricot bean, rinsed
- ½ cup vegetable stock
- Lemon wedges, to serve

Directions

1. Preheat the grill and grease its grilling grate.
2. Arrange all the vegetables on the grates and grill them until golden from both sides.
3. Meanwhile, cook beans and garlic in the stock and let it simmer for 10 minutes.
4. Mash the beans in this mixture roughly with a masher.
5. Spread this beans mash in the serving plates and place the grilled vegetables over it.
6. Garnish with lemon wedges, coriander, oil and black pepper to serve.

Nutrition

Calories: 372 Carbs: 60.6g Fats: 15.4g Proteins: 12.3g Sodium: 206mg Sugar: 27.8g

Sandwiches and Wraps Recipes

Avocado and Egg Sandwich

Serves: 4
Prep Time: 15 mins

Avocado and egg sandwiches are always refreshing to serve as a snack or breakfast.

Ingredients

- 2 tablespoons olive oil
- 1 teaspoon lemon juice
- 1 whole wheat bagel, sliced

- 1 avocado, mashed
- 2 eggs
- ¼ teaspoon black pepper
- ¼ teaspoon salt

Directions
1. Scoop out some material from inside of the bagel slices to make 1-inch wide hole.
2. Brush the prepared slice with olive oil and sear in a heated pan.
3. Meanwhile, mix avocado flesh with lemon juice.
4. Spread the avocado mixture in the hole of the toasted bagel.
5. Crack an egg at the center of each slice and season it with salt and black pepper.
6. Place them in the baking sheet and bake for about 4 minutes to serve.

Nutrition
Calories: 257 Carbs: 16.9g Fats: 19.4g Proteins: 6.5g Sodium: 294mg Sugar: 2.7g

Mediterranean Veggie Wrap

Serves: 2
Prep Time: 15 mins
These veggie wraps are best to serve to all the vegetarians, making an appealing delight for the dinner table.

Ingredients
- ¼ cup red onions, sliced
- ½ small zucchini, sliced
- ¼ cup hummus
- 2 tablespoons feta cheese, crumbled
- 1 tablespoon black olives, sliced
- ½ teaspoon olive oil
- ½ medium red bell pepper, sliced
- 2 whole grain tortillas
- ½ cup baby spinach
- 1 teaspoon dried oregano

Directions
1. Heat oil in a small skillet and add zucchini, red onions, and bell pepper.
2. Sauté for about 5 minutes and keep aside.
3. Heat tortillas in another skillet and spread half of the hummus in each tortilla.
4. Equally divide spinach between wraps and layer with sautéed vegetables.
5. Sprinkle with olives, feta cheese, and oregano.
6. Fold the edges of the tortillas to roll up and serve warm.

Nutrition
Calories: 265 Carbs: 35.4g Fats: 10.4g Proteins: 10g Sodium: 590mg Sugar: 5.1g

Loaded Mediterranean Veggie Sandwich

Serves: 4
Prep Time: 25 mins
This is my most favorite veggie sandwich, as it is light, healthy and flavorful.

Ingredients
- 6 tablespoons cilantro jalapeno hummus
- ½ cup sprouts
- 4 slices whole wheat bread
- 2 whole leaves fresh lettuce
- 4 whole tomatoes, thinly sliced
- 2 red onions, thinly sliced
- 4 Peppadew peppers, chopped
- 4 whole cucumbers, thinly sliced
- 4 tablespoons feta cheese, crumbled

Directions
1. Toast the bread and spread hummus on both the slices.
2. Layer with sprouts, lettuce, tomato, feta cheese, red onion, cucumber, and peppadew peppers.
3. Slice the sandwich and serve immediately.

Nutrition

Calories: 273 Carbs: 48.2g Fats: 5.2g Proteins: 11.1g Sodium: 433mg Sugar: 20.6g

Couscous and Chicken Tender Wrap

Serves: 4
Prep Time: 40 mins
This wrap is stuffed with couscous and chicken tenders with a healthy dose of fresh herbs and a hit of lemon.

Ingredients
- ⅓ cup couscous, whole-wheat
- ½ cup water
- 1 cup fresh parsley, chopped
- ¼ cup lemon juice
- 2 teaspoons garlic, minced
- ½ cup fresh mint, chopped
- 3 tablespoons extra-virgin olive oil
- Salt, to taste

Directions
1. Boil water in a pan and add couscous.
2. Remove from heat and fluff with a fork.
3. Meanwhile, mix together mint, parsley, lemon juice, garlic, oil, salt, and black pepper in a small bowl.
4. Mix together chicken tenders, 1 tablespoon of the mint mixture and some salt in a medium bowl.
5. Cook chicken tenders in a large nonstick skillet and cook for about 4 minutes on each side.
6. Dish out and cut into bite-sized pieces.
7. Stir in the remaining parsley mixture, tomato and cucumber into the couscous to serve.

Nutrition
Calories: 510 Carbs: 55g Fats: 18g Proteins: 32g Sodium: 726mg Sugar: 5g

Mediterranean Grilled Cheese Sandwich

Serves: 1
Prep Time: 15 mins
A Mediterranean inspired grilled cheese sandwich is deliciously melty and gooey on the inside.

Ingredients
- 1 tablespoon extra-virgin olive oil, divided
- 1 oz. Feta cheese, crumbled
- 2 sourdough bread slices
- 2 oz. whole milk Mozzarella cheese, shredded
- 2 cups fresh spinach
- 2 teaspoons fresh basil, chopped
- Black pepper, to taste
- 4 Roma tomatoes, sliced
- 2 tablespoons black olives, diced
- 1 tablespoon red onion, finely chopped
- ¼ teaspoon garlic, finely minced

Directions
1. Heat half of olive oil in a non-stick skillet and add spinach and garlic.
2. Sauté for about 30 seconds and stir in basil.
3. Spread feta and Mozzarella cheese over one slice of bread.
4. Layer with tomatoes, followed by spinach mixture, olives, and red onions.
5. Sprinkle with black pepper and top with the other slice of bread.
6. Heat remaining olive oil in the skillet and add sandwich.
7. Cook for about 4 minutes on each side until bottom is golden brown.
8. Dish out and serve immediately.

Nutrition
Calories: 642 Carbs: 81g Fats: 37g Proteins: 34g Sodium: 1628mg Sugar: 7g

Mediterranean Fish Wraps

Serves: 4
Prep Time: 15 mins
These are well-cooked Mediterranean fish wraps that can guarantee both health and good taste.

Ingredients
- 4 ounces feta cheese, crumbled
- ½ cup jarred roasted red peppers, chopped
- 4 cups fish, cooked and shredded
- ½ cup plain Greek yogurt
- ½ cup black olives, chopped
- 2 teaspoons fresh lemon juice
- ¼ teaspoon black pepper

- 4 cups baby arugula
- 1 teaspoon fresh lemon zest
- ½ teaspoon salt
- 4 (12-inch) flour tortillas, whole wheat

Directions
1. Mix together chicken, yogurt, feta, lemon juice, red peppers, lemon zest, olives, salt, and black pepper in a bowl.
2. Divide the baby arugula in the tortillas and spoon the chicken mixture in the center of the tortilla.
3. Tightly roll up and cut in half to serve.

Nutrition
Calories: 441
Carbs: 41.8g
Fats: 20.9g
Proteins: 23.8g
Sodium: 1313mg
Sugar: 3g

Pita Sandwich

Serves: 2
Prep Time: 25 mins
Pesto and hummus make this version of a pita sandwich special.

Ingredients
- 4 tablespoons hummus
- 2 pita breads
- 2 tablespoons pesto
- ¼ cup cucumber, sliced and quartered
- ¼ cup parsley, chopped
- 4 tablespoons feta cheese, crumbled
- 10 black olives, sliced
- 10 cherry tomatoes, halved

Directions
1. Heat Pita bread in a pan and dish out.
2. Spread hummus on the top of each pita and top with pesto.
3. Layer with cherry tomatoes, parsley, black olives, feta cheese, and cucumber.
4. Fold and cut in slices to serve.

Nutrition
Calories: 469
Carbs: 65.4g
Fats: 17.6g
Proteins: 17.7g
Sodium: 958mg
Sugar: 19g

Mushroom Veggies Wrap

Serves: 4
Prep Time: 35 mins
This is a great wrap for lunch or dinner and can be made with all sorts of leftovers.

Ingredients
- 1 zucchini, sliced
- ¼ pound fresh mushrooms, sliced
- 1 red onion, sliced
- 1 eggplant, sliced
- 1 red bell pepper, sliced
- Salt and black pepper, to taste
- ¼ cup goat cheese
- 1 large avocado, sliced
- 1 tablespoon olive oil
- 4 whole grain tortillas
- ¼ cup basil pesto

Directions
1. Put the onions, eggplant, zucchini, bell pepper and mushrooms in a bowl.
2. Drizzle with the olive oil and season with salt, and black pepper.
3. Heat a skillet and add the seasoned vegetables.
4. Cook for about 10 minutes and spread 1 tablespoon each of pesto and goat cheese in each tortilla.
5. Put the sliced avocados and mixed veggies in the tortillas.
6. Roll tightly into a wrap and serve.

Nutrition
Calories: 436 Carbs: 48.4g Fats: 26.3g Proteins: 14.6g Sodium: 433mg Sugar: 8g

Mediterranean Pressed Sandwich

Serves: 4
Prep Time: 10 mins

This is a pressed sandwich filled with all the perkiest flavors of the Mediterranean cuisine.

Ingredients
- 1 garlic clove, cut lengthwise
- 8 kalamata olives, pitted
- ¼ pound green beans, blanched
- 2 small baguettes, cut in half lengthwise
- 2 sundried tomatoes
- ½ medium red bell pepper, roasted
- 1 tomato, cored and seeded
- 1 tablespoon olive oil
- Salt and black pepper, to taste
- 2 anchovy fillets
- 1 teaspoon lemon juice

Directions
1. Mix together all the ingredients in a food processor and pulse until chunky.
2. Stir in the lemon juice, olive oil, salt and black pepper.
3. Spread the mixture in each baguette and wrap each sandwich in waxed paper tightly.
4. Place a heavy object on top of the sandwiches and press down firmly for one hour before serving.

Nutrition
Calories: 111
Carbs: 14.2g
Fats: 5.1g
Proteins: 3.5g
Sodium: 278mg
Sugar: 2.4g

Pizza and Pasta Recipes

Garlic Bread Pizzas

Serves: 4

Prep Time: 25 mins
The flour crust of these bread pizzas is topped with mozzarella mixed tomato and basil toppings.

Ingredients For the dough
- 1 sachet fast-action yeast
- 1 pound strong whole wheat flour, plus extra for rolling
- 1 teaspoon salt
- 2 tablespoons olive oil

For the topping:
- 2 garlic cloves, crushed
- ¼ cup almond butter, softened
- 1½ cups mozzarella, drained
- 1 handful basil leaves, roughly chopped
- 1 teaspoon balsamic vinegar
- 4 tomatoes, roughly chopped
- 1 tablespoon extra-virgin olive oil

Directions
1. Preheat the oven to 320 degrees F and grease 2 baking sheets.
2. Knead together all the ingredients for the dough in a bowl and roll out into eight equal pieces.
3. Mix together garlic and melted butter in a bowl and pour over the dough.
4. Arrange these pieces into the baking sheets and top with mozzarella cheese.
5. Transfer into the oven and bake for about 15 minutes.
6. Top with the remaining ingredients and immediately serve.

Nutrition
Calories: 629 Carbs: 92.2g Fats: 21.8g Proteins: 16g Sodium: 735mg Sugar: 3.6g

Mediterranean Olive Oil Pasta

Serves: 4
Prep Time: 25 mins
This Mediterranean Olive Oil Pasta is a family favorite and best for all occasions.

Ingredients
- ½ cup olive oil
- Salt, to taste
- 1 pound thin spaghetti, boiled
- 4 garlic cloves, crushed
- 1 cup fresh parsley, chopped
- 3 scallions, chopped
- 6 oz. marinated artichoke hearts, drained
- ¼ cup feta cheese, crumbled
- 15 fresh basil leaves, torn
- 2 tablespoons red pepper flakes, crushed
- 12 oz. grape tomatoes, halved
- 1 teaspoon black pepper
- ¼ cup pitted olives, halved
- 1 lemon zest

Directions
1. Put olive oil in a skillet and add garlic and salt.
2. Sauté for 30 seconds and add tomatoes, parsley and scallions.
3. Cook for about 2 minutes and add boiled pasta.
4. Toss well and season with black pepper.
5. Garnish with feta cheese and basil leaves to serve.

Nutrition
Calories: 520 Carbs: 47.4g Fats: 33.8g Proteins: 10.6g Sodium: 396mg Sugar: 4.8g

Easy Tomato Pizzas

Serves: 4
Prep Time: 22 mins
As the crust is loaded with nothing but tomatoes and cheese, so the tomato lovers will instantly fall for these mini pizzas.

Ingredients For the dough
- 1 sachet fast-action yeast
- 1½ cups warm water
- 1 pound bread flour, plus more to dust
- 2 tablespoons olive oil

For the topping
- 8 tomatoes
- ½ cup Parmesan cheese, grated

- 5 tablespoons roast tomato sauce
- ½ cup goat's cheese, grated

Directions
1. Preheat the oven to 390 degrees F and grease 2 baking sheets.
2. Mix yeast with flour in a bowl and stir in in water and oil.
3. Knead this dough well for 2 minutes and cover the dough with a plastic sheet.
4. Keep it at a warm place for 2 hours and knead the dough into eight equal balls.
5. Arrange these balls into 2 baking sheets and layer with sauce, tomato slices, parmesan, and seasoning.
6. Transfer in the oven and bake for about 12 minutes.
7. Dish out to serve and enjoy.

Nutrition
Calories: 522 Carbs: 97.1g Fats: 8.6g Proteins: 14.1g Sodium: 115mg Sugar: 7.6g

Mediterranean Whole Wheat Pasta

Serves: 4
Prep Time: 20 mins
This delicious blend of many robust ingredients will explode with flavor in your mouth.

Ingredients
- 6 ounces whole wheat noodles
- 4 garlic cloves, minced
- 1 (14-ounce) can quartered artichoke hearts
- 3 tablespoons olive oil
- ½ teaspoon red pepper flakes, crushed
- ¼ cup fresh Italian parsley, chopped
- Salt, to taste
- 2 cups cherry tomatoes
- 1 (6-ounce) can whole black olives, pitted
- Black pepper, to taste
- ¼ cup lemon juice, freshly squeezed
- ¼ cup Parmesan cheese, freshly grated

Directions
1. Boil spaghetti pasta in salted water until al dente.
2. Drain under cold water and keep aside.

3. Put olive oil to an iron skillet along with tomatoes, garlic, salt, black pepper and red pepper flakes.
4. Sauté for about 2 minutes and add artichokes, olives and lemon juice.
5. Cook for another 2 minutes and add pasta.
6. Adjust seasoning with salt and black pepper.
7. Garnish with parsley and parmesan cheese to serve.

Nutrition
Calories: 483 Carbs: 47.4g Fats: 29.7g Proteins: 10.9g Sodium: 258mg Sugar: 4.1g

Goat's Cheese Pizza

Serves: 10
Prep Time: 55 mins
This Goat's Cheese pizza is great to make when you don't have enough to afford cooking or baking of any sort.

Ingredients
- 7 oz. marinated grilled yellow and red bell peppers in olive oil
- 2/3 cup watercress
- 1 handful black olives
- 1 round focaccia loaf, halved
- 3 tablespoons pesto
- 4 oz. soft goat's cheese, crumbled

Directions
1. Put the bell peppers in a colander to drain them keeping their oil preserved.
2. Top the loaf halves with a teaspoon of pesto over cut side.
3. Divide cheese, watercress and bell pepper over each loaf half.
4. Mix the remaining pesto with 1 tablespoon pepper oil.
5. Drizzle this oil over the focaccia loafs and garnish with olives to serve.

Nutrition
Calories: 256
Carbs: 28.7g
Fats: 12.2g
Proteins: 10.6g
Sodium: 370mg
Sugar: 2.5g

Pasta with Sautéed Spinach and Garlic

Serves: 4
Prep Time: 20 mins
The spinach cuts down some of the super-strong garlic flavor in this pasta recipe.

Ingredients
- ½ cup extra-virgin olive oil
- 2 teaspoons oregano, dried
- ½ pound uncooked spaghetti
- 10 garlic cloves, chopped
- 1 teaspoon basil, dried
- 1 teaspoon balsamic vinegar
- ½ cup parmesan cheese, grated
- 10 ounces fresh spinach, stems removed
- Salt and black pepper, to taste

Directions
1. Boil spaghetti pasta in salted water until al dente.
2. Drain under cold water and keep aside.
3. Sauté garlic, basil and oregano in olive oil for about 1 minute.
4. Add spinach and sauté for another 3 minutes.
5. Turn off the heat and add balsamic vinegar.
6. Stir in pasta and garnish with parmesan cheese to serve warm.

Nutrition
Calories: 253
Carbs: 31.9g
Fats: 12.4g
Proteins: 13g
Sodium: 478mg
Sugar: 4g

Mediterranean Artichoke Pizza

Serves: 6
Prep Time: 20 mins
Artichokes take this Mediterranean Pizza to the highest pillar, having highest levels of healthy anti-aging and disease-fighting antioxidants.

Ingredients
- 1 cup pesto sauce
- 1 cup sun-dried tomato
- ½ cup kalamata olives
- 4 ounces mozzarella cheese
- 1 pizza dough crust
- 1 cup artichoke heart
- 1 cup spinach leaves, wilted
- 4 ounces feta cheese

Directions
1. Preheat the oven to 350 degrees F and grease a baking pan.
2. Spread the pizza dough crust in the baking pan and add pesto sauce.
3. Top with olives, artichoke hearts, spinach leaves and sun-dried tomatoes.
4. Sprinkle with cheese and transfer into the oven.
5. Bake for about 10 minutes and dish out to serve.

Nutrition
Calories: 406
Carbs: 41.3g
Fats: 14.1g
Proteins: 30g
Sodium: 871mg
Sugar: 4.3g

Mediterranean Cauliflower Pizza

Serves: 6
Prep Time: 35 mins
Everybody would really enjoy it. Add spicy garlic or red pepper flakes for extra spice.

Ingredients
- 1½ tablespoons olive oil, divided
- 1 lemon, sliced
- ⅓ cup black olives, pitted and sliced
- 1 cup mozzarella cheese, shredded
- ¼ cup fresh basil, slivered
- 1 medium head cauliflower, diced
- ¼ teaspoon salt
- 6 sun-dried tomatoes, chopped and drained

- 1 large egg, lightly beaten
- ½ teaspoon dried oregano
- Black pepper, to taste

Directions
1. Preheat the oven to 350 degrees F and grease a baking sheet.
2. Process cauliflower in a food processor until shredded.
3. Add 1 tablespoon oil and salt to a skillet and add cauliflower.
4. Sauté for about 10 minutes and dish out in a bowl.
5. Mix together olives, tomatoes, egg, oregano, cheese, and lemon slices in a bowl.
6. Add this mixture to the cooled cauliflower and pour into the baking sheet.
7. Transfer in the oven and bake for 14 minutes.
8. Garnish with basil and serve warm.

Nutrition
Calories: 227 Carbs: 18.3g Fats: 35.5g Proteins: 7.2g Sodium: 1248mg Sugar: 2.9g

Margherita Pizza

Serves: 10
Prep Time: 35 mins
This Margherita pizza gives you abundant fats to utilize as a body fuel.

Ingredients
- ¼ cup flour
- 1 batch pizza dough
- 2 tablespoons olive oil
- 3 Roma tomatoes, sliced ¼ inch thick
- ½ teaspoon sea salt
- ½ cup fresh basil leaves, chopped
- ½ cup canned tomatoes, crushed
- 6 ounces fresh mozzarella, sliced

Directions
1. Preheat the oven to 450 degrees F and grease a pizza pan.
2. Roll the pizza dough into a half thick sheet and place in a pizza pan.
3. Poke some holes using a fork and bake for about 5 minutes.
4. Add crushed tomatoes and olives to the baked crust.
5. Top with tomatoes, salt and mozzarella slices.
6. Garnish with basil and bake for about 15 minutes.

7. Top the pizza with the tomato slices and season with the salt.
8. Broil for about 3 minutes and serve.

Nutrition
Calories: 224
Carbs: 19g
Fats: 35.3g
Proteins: 2.6g
Sodium: 2073mg
Sugar: 4.8g

Fish and Seafood Recipes

Mixed Seafood Stew

Serves: 4
Prep Time: 20 mins
This stew has a variety of seafood, including clam juice, fish, scallops and shrimp, which is cooked in tomato-based sauce.

Ingredients
- 1 medium onion, finely chopped
- 1 tablespoon olive oil
- 1½ teaspoons garlic, minced and divided
- ½ pound plum tomatoes, seeded and diced
- 1 teaspoon lemon peel, grated
- ¼ teaspoon red pepper flakes, crushed
- 1/3 cup white wine
- 1 tablespoon tomato paste
- Salt, to taste
- 1 oz. red snapper fillets, cut into 1-inch cubes
- 1 pound shrimp, peeled and deveined
- ½ pound sea scallops
- 1 cup clam juice
- 1/3 cup fresh parsley, minced
- 1/3 cup mayonnaise, reduced-fat

Directions
1. Heat cooking oil in a Dutch oven on medium heat and stir in garlic and onions.
2. Sauté until soft and add tomatoes, lemon peel and pepper flakes.

3. Sauté for 2 minutes and stir in wine, salt, tomato paste, and clam juice.
4. Boil this mixture then reduce it to a simmer.
5. Cover the lid and cook for 10 minutes.
6. Gently toss in shrimps, scallops, parsley and fish.
7. Cook, covered for 10 more minutes and garnish with garlic and mayonnaise to serve.

Nutrition
Calories: 390 Carbs: 20.1g Fats: 15.3g Proteins: 39g Sodium: 673mg Sugar: 7.3g

Sauce Dipped Mussels

Serves: 2
Prep Time: 35 mins
This is a rare mussel's recipe, which is cooked into such a delicious, yet simple, meal.

Ingredients
- 2 tablespoons olive oil
- 1 red or green chili, deseeded and chopped
- 2 ripe tomatoes, soaked, drained and diced
- 1 garlic clove, minced
- 1 shallot, finely diced
- 1 glass dry white wine
- 1 pinch sugar
- 1 handful basil leaves
- 1 teaspoon tomato paste
- 1 pound mussels, cleaned

Directions
1. Heat olive oil in a wok and stir in garlic, chili, and shallots.
2. Sauté for about 3 minutes and add seasonings, sugar, wine, and tomatoes.
3. Cook for about 2 minutes and add mussels.
4. Cover with a lid and cook for about 4 minutes.
5. Garnish with basil leaves to serve.

Nutrition
Calories: 320
Carbs: 19.4g
Fats: 17.8g
Proteins: 20.3g
Sodium: 537mg
Sugar: 6.8g
Calories320

Squid Oyster Medley

Serves: 4
Prep Time: 55 mins
This squid oyster medley is the perfect option as it pairs unique ingredients together in a tasty combination.
Ingredients
- 4 garlic cloves, minced
- 1½ cups chicken stock
- 10 baby squids, cleaned
- 1½ cups milk
- 1 large carrot, chopped
- ¼ cup tomato paste
- ¼ bunch tarragon, fresh
- 4 tablespoons olive oil, divided
- 1 tomato, chopped
- ¼ bunch parsley, fresh
- ½ teaspoon black peppercorns
- 3 baby fennel bulbs, halved
- 10 fresh mussels
- 3 sprigs parsley, for garnish
- ½ tablespoon saffron threads, loosely packed
- ¼ bunch fresh thyme, chopped
- 3 (6 ounce) fillets fresh sea bass
- 1 small onion, chopped
- ½ cup dry white wine
- ¼ bunch fresh thyme
- 3 cloves garlic, minced
- 5 fresh oysters in shells, scrubbed well
- Salt and black pepper, to taste
- 1 bay leaf
- ¼ cup oil-packed sun-dried tomatoes, drained and cut into strips
- 10 clams

Directions
1. Soak the squids in the milk for 5 hours and drain the milk.
2. Heat half of oil in a cooking pan and add tomatoes, half of the fennels, carrots, garlic, and onions.
3. Sauté for about 8 minutes and stir in tomato paste.
4. Cook for about 10 minutes and pour in the wine.
5. Bring to a boil and add saffron, tarragon, thyme, stock, bay leaves, parsley, and peppercorns.
6. Cook for about 12 minutes and strain the stock.
7. Discard all the vegetables and dish out in a bowl.
8. Heat the remaining oil in the same pot and add garlic.
9. Sauté for about 30 seconds and stir in the tomatoes and remaining fennel.
10. Cook for about 2 minutes and bring to a boil.
11. Add the oysters to the pot and cook, covered for about 5 minutes.
12. Stir in the mussels and clams and cook for about 3 minutes.
13. Add drained squid and cook for another 1 minute.
14. Meanwhile, sear the fish fillets in a skillet for about 4 minutes on each side.
15. Serve topped with fish fillets and garnished with parsley.

Nutrition
Calories: 414
Carbs: 25.6g
Fats: 11.3g
Proteins: 43.2g
Sodium: 696mg
Sugar: 10.2g

Crusty Grilled Mussels

Serves: 2
Prep Time: 15 mins
These mussels are seasoned to get a fine taste with nothing but herbs and lemon zest.

Ingredients
- 1 cup toasted bread crumbs
- 2 tablespoons garlic and parsley butter
- Fresh herbs, to garnish
- 1 pound mussels, rinsed and debearded
- 1 lemon zest
- Chopped tomato, to garnish

Directions
1. Boil mussels in a water in a large pot for about 3 minutes.
2. Preheat the grill and grease a baking sheet.
3. Mix zest and bread crumbs in a bowl.
4. Drizzle butter on top of the mussels and arrange them shell side down on the baking sheet.
5. Top the mussels with bread crumbs mixture and transfer on the grill.
6. Cover the grill for about 4 minutes and allow to cook.
7. Garnish with tomato and parsley to serve.

Nutrition
Calories: 510
Carbs: 47.3g
Fats: 19.5g
Proteins: 34.3g
Sodium: 1126mg
Sugar: 3.4g

Seafood Garlic Couscous

Serves: 4
Prep Time: 30 mins
This combination of seafood, garlic and couscous is good for all the special diet and health plans.

Ingredients
- ½ pound raw shrimp, peeled, deveined and coarsely chopped
- 4 scallions, sliced
- ½ cup fresh parsley, chopped
- 2 tablespoons olive oil
- 2 (5.4-oz.) boxes garlic-flavored couscous, boiled and drained
- 1 pound codfish, cut into 1-inch pieces
- ½ pound bay scallops
- ½ cup fresh chives, chopped
- Salt and black pepper, to taste
- Hot sauce, to taste

Directions
1. Mix shrimps with codfish, scallions, scallops, parsley, chives, salt, and black pepper in a bowl.
2. Heat oil in a deep wok and add seafood mixture.
3. Sauté until golden and stir in hot sauce.

4. Lower the heat and cover with a lid.
5. Divide the couscous into the serving plates and top evenly with the fish mixture.
6. Serve immediately.

Nutrition
Calories: 476
Carbs: 68g
Fats: 9g
Proteins: 32.9g
Sodium: 294mg
Sugar: 0.8g

Lobster Rice Paella

Serves: 2
Prep Time: 40 mins
Lobster's tail meat has this amazing taste that is nicely complemented when cooked with rice paella.

Ingredients
- 1 small onion, chopped
- 2 garlic cloves, chopped
- ½ teaspoon sweet Spanish paprika
- 1½ tablespoons olive oil
- 3 oz. French green beans
- ¼ cup fresh parsley, chopped
- Water, as required
- 2 small lobster tails
- 1 cup Spanish rice, soaked overnight and drained
- 1 large pinch of Spanish saffron threads soaked in ½ cup water
- ½ teaspoon cayenne pepper
- ¼ teaspoon Aleppo pepper flakes
- 1 large Roma tomato, finely chopped
- ½ pound prawns, peeled and deveined
- Salt, to taste

Directions
1. Boil lobster in water for 2 minutes and transfer to an ice bath immediately.
2. Remove the meat from its shell and cut into small sized chunks.
3. Heat 3 tablespoons of oil in a skillet and add onions.
4. Sauté for about 2 minutes and add rice.

5. Cook for about 3 minutes and add garlic and lobsters.
6. Stir in paprika, saffron, salt and black pepper and add tomatoes and green beans.
7. Cover with a lid and reduce the heat to low.
8. Allow it to cook for about 18 minutes and add shrimps.
9. Cover again and cook for about 14 minutes.
10. Stir in parsley and lobster chunks to serve immediately.

Nutrition
Calories: 464 Carbs: 40.3g Fats: 13.1g Proteins: 30.4g Sodium: 1013mg Sugar: 4.7g

Fish and Vegetable Parcels

Serves: 2
Prep Time: 35 mins
These parcels have many of the extra secret ingredients, including olives, capers, and potatoes unlike simple fish packets.

Ingredients
- 1 teaspoon olive oil
- 1 small lemon zest, finely grated
- 10 black olives
- 2 fresh rosemary sprigs
- 1¼ cups baby potatoes, scrubbed
- 2 (6 oz.) firm haddock fillets
- 2 teaspoons sun-dried tomato paste
- 2 teaspoons lemon juice
- 1 tablespoon capers, rinsed

Directions
1. Preheat the oven to 325 degrees F and grease 2 baking sheets.
2. Boil potatoes in a salt mixed water in a large pot and transfer in a colander to drain well.
3. Place one fish fillet in each of the baking sheet and drizzle with lemon juice, tomato paste, seasonings and lemon zest.
4. Arrange capers, potatoes and olives on the sides of fillets and cover the fillets with rosemary sprigs.
5. Transfer in the oven and bake for about 25 minutes.
6. Dish out and serve immediately.

Nutrition
Calories: 269
Carbs: 9.1g
Fats: 6.7g
Proteins: 42.8g
Sodium: 477mg
Sugar: 1.5g

Seafood with Couscous Salad

Serves: 2
Prep Time: 35 mins
The best part about this seafood recipe is that the cooked fish is served with vegetable mixed couscous salad.

Ingredients
- 2 lemons, 1 zested and juiced and the other cut into wedges
- 7 oz. cherry tomatoes
- 2 tablespoons balsamic vinegar
- 2 tablespoons pitted black olives, halved
- 2 white fish fillets
- 1 red chili, sliced
- 1 small bunch basil, shredded
- 4 oz. couscous
- ½ cucumber, diced

Directions
1. Preheat the oven to 375 degrees F and grease a baking sheet.
2. Place the fish in the baking sheet and add basil, seasonings, sliced chilies and half of the lemon juice and zest.
3. Surround the fillets with tomatoes and transfer in the oven.
4. Bake for about 20 minutes and dish out.
5. Meanwhile, soak couscous in boiled water for about 20 minutes and drain well.
6. Mix together couscous, basil, tomatoes, cucumber, olives, lemon zest and juice in a bowl.
7. Serve the baked fish with the couscous salad and enjoy.

Nutrition
Calories: 538 Carbs: 56.8g Fats: 13.3g Proteins: 47.1g Sodium: 188mg Sugar: 5.5g

Saffron Fish Gratins

Serves: 6
Prep Time: 45 mins
The gratin is usually a cheese-rich, crumbly bake made by using a saffron fish prawn mixture.

Ingredients
- 1 large onion, thinly sliced
- 3 large garlic cloves, finely sliced
- ½ cup white wine
- 3 tablespoons olive oil
- 1 fennel bulb, trimmed and thinly sliced
- 1 heaped teaspoon coriander seeds, lightly crushed
- 2 (14 oz.) cans chopped tomatoes with herbs
- 1 pinch saffron
- 1 tablespoon lemon juice
- 2 pounds mixed skinless fish fillets, cut into chunks
- ¼ cup parmesan cheese, finely grated
- Green salad, to serve
- 2 tablespoons tomato purée
- 1 bay leaf
- 1 bunch parsley, leaves roughly chopped
- 1¾ cups raw king prawns, peeled
- ¼ cup panko breadcrumbs

Directions
1. Preheat the oven to 375 degrees F and grease a baking dish.
2. Heat oil in a large nonstick pan and add fennel, garlic, onions and coriander seeds.
3. Sauté for about 5 minutes and pour in wine, saffron, tomatoes, tomato puree and bay leaf.
4. Cook for about 15 minutes and add tomatoes mixture, prawns, and fish chunks.
5. Cook for about 5 minutes and transfer the mixture a baking dish.
6. Mix together breadcrumbs, parsley, cheese and black pepper and top it on the fish mixture.
7. Transfer in the oven and bake for about 20 minutes to serve.

Nutrition
Calories: 501 Carbs: 38.7g Fats: 26.4g Proteins: 27.5g Sodium: 880mg Sugar: 3.8g

Vegetable Main Dishes Recipes

Griddled Vegetable and Feta Tart

Serves: 4
Prep Time: 40 mins

This is no ordinary vegetable tart, rather the phyllo sheet is baked with charred and grilled veggies.

Ingredients
- 1 aubergine, sliced
- 2 red onions, chunked
- 2 tablespoons olive oil
- 2 zucchinis, sliced
- 3 large sheets filo pastry
- 1 tablespoon balsamic vinegar
- 1 teaspoon dried oregano
- 12 cherry tomatoes, halved
- ½ cup feta cheese, crumbled

Directions
1. Preheat the oven to 375 degrees F and line a baking dish with filo pastry.
2. Heat oil into a griddle pan and add aubergines.
3. Grill until charred and dish out in a plate.
4. Grill the onions and zucchinis in the pan.
5. Place the charred vegetables, tomatoes, and seasonings in the baking dish.
6. Sprinkle with feta cheese and oregano and transfer in the oven.
7. Bake for about 20 minutes and remove from the oven to serve.

Nutrition
Calories: 482 Carbs: 50.8g Fats: 26.5g Proteins: 14g Sodium: 914mg Sugar: 22.6g

Mediterranean Gnocchi

Serves: 4
Prep Time: 15 mins

The spongy and soft gnocchi is cooked with grilled and charred vegetables.

Ingredients

- 7 oz. chargrilled vegetables (aubergines, peppers, semi-dried tomatoes, and artichokes)
- 1 handful basil leaves
- 14 oz. gnocchi, boiled and drained
- 2 tablespoons red pesto
- Parmesan cheese, to serve

Directions
1. Put the gnocchi to a pan along with a splash of water.
2. Stir in charred vegetables, red pesto, basil leaves, and parmesan cheese.
3. Dish out and serve.

Nutrition
Calories: 223
Carbs: 38.6g
Fats: 4.5g
Proteins: 5.6g
Sodium: 644mg
Sugar: 1.6g

Parmesan Roasted Broccoli

Serves: 4
Prep Time: 35 mins

The cheese parmesan broccoli bake is a nice option to serve the broccoli and the vegetables actually taste tempting.

Ingredients
- 2 tablespoons olive oil
- ½ cup Parmesan cheese, grated
- 1 lemon, zested
- Pinch of flaky sea salt
- 1 pound broccoli florets, cut into bite-sized pieces
- Salt, to taste
- 2 tablespoons balsamic vinegar
- Pinch of red pepper flakes

Directions
1. Preheat the oven to 400 degrees F and grease a baking sheet.
2. Season the broccoli florets with salt and arrange on the baking sheet.
3. Bake for about 15 minutes and sprinkle with parmesan cheese.

4. Bake these florets again for 10 minutes and season with lemon zest, salt, red pepper flakes, and balsamic vinegar to serve.

Nutrition
Calories: 146
Carbs: 8.5g
Fats: 10.4g
Proteins: 7.7g
Sodium: 167mg
Sugar: 2.4g

Baked Goat Cheese with Tomato Sauce

Serves: 4
Prep Time: 30 mins
The ramekins are filled with well-cooked tomato sauce and topped with cheese to make a delicious meal.

Ingredients
- ½ cup white onions, finely chopped
- 1¼ tablespoons fresh basil, chopped
- 1½ teaspoons white wine vinegar
- ½ teaspoon salt
- Whole grain baguette, to serve
- 1 tablespoon olive oil
- 2 medium garlic cloves, pressed or minced
- ¼ teaspoon red pepper flakes
- ¼ teaspoon dried oregano
- 1 can (15 ounces) crushed tomatoes
- Black pepper, to taste
- 4 ounces goat cheese

Directions
1. Preheat the oven to 375 degrees F and grease 4 ramekins.
2. Pour oil in a pan and add onions.
3. Sauté for about 3 minutes and add basil, red pepper flakes, oregano, and garlic.
4. Cook for about 1 minute and add white wine vinegar, tomatoes, salt, and black pepper.
5. Cover with a lid and cook for about 10 minutes.
6. Divide this mixture into the ramekins and sprinkle with cheese.
7. Arrange the ramekins in a baking tray and transfer in the oven.

8. Bake for about 15 minutes and top with olive oil and basil to serve.

Nutrition
Calories: 112 Carbs: 8.2g Fats: 8.1g Proteins: 4.3g Sodium: 109mg Sugar: 2.4g

Roasted Vegetable Tabbouleh

Serves: 4
Prep Time: 35 mins
Tabbouleh has quite a refreshing taste, and this dish is full of fibers and all the essential nutrients.

Ingredients
- 3 medium carrots, chopped
- 1 (16-ounce) can garbanzo beans, rinsed and drained
- ¾ cup bulgur, boiled and drained
- 1 small red onion, chopped
- ½ cup fresh parsley, chopped
- 3 tablespoons lemon juice
- 2 tablespoons olive oil
- ¼ teaspoon black pepper
- ⅛ teaspoon salt
- ½ teaspoon lemon peel, finely shredded
- 2 tablespoons water
- 2 teaspoons fresh thyme, snipped
- 1 medium tomato, chopped

Directions
1. Preheat the oven to 400 degrees F and grease a baking dish.
2. Arrange carrots and onions in a baking dish and drizzle with olive oil.
3. Bake for about 25 minutes and dish out in a bowl.
4. Add bulgur, lemon peel, pepper, salt, parsley, lemon juice, and garbanzo to the baked veggies bowl to serve.

Nutrition
Calories: 370 Carbs: 58.7g Fats: 10.6g Proteins: 14.1g Sodium: 57mg Sugar: 9.6g

Vegan Pesto Spaghetti Squash

Serves: 4
Prep Time: 1 hour
Spaghetti squash is a nice alternative to carb-rich pasta meal since it is made out of cooked squash.

Ingredients
- 4 tablespoons extra-virgin olive oil, divided
- ½ cup sun-dried tomatoes, julienned
- 1 (3-pounds) spaghetti squash, halved lengthwise and seeded
- 8 ounces cremini mushrooms, sliced
- ½ teaspoon salt, divided
- 2 garlic cloves, coarsely chopped
- 3 tablespoons lemon juice
- ½ teaspoon black pepper
- 1 cup packed fresh basil leaves
- ⅓ cup unsalted raw cashews
- 2 teaspoons nutritional yeast

Directions
1. Preheat the oven to 400 degrees F and grease a baking sheet.
2. Arrange the squash on the baking sheet and bake for about 45 minutes.
3. Sauté mushrooms, tomatoes and salt in 1 tablespoon oil in a pan for about 5 minutes.
4. Blend 3 tablespoons of oil with basil, cashews, yeast, lemon juice, garlic, salt, and black pepper.
5. Scrape the flesh of the baked squash to get thin spaghetti.
6. Place the spaghetti in a colander to drain all the liquid.
7. Divide the squash spaghetti into the serving plates and top with mushrooms and basil sauce to serve.

Nutrition
Calories: 245 Carbs: 15g Fats: 20g Proteins: 5.4g Sodium: 450mg Sugar: 4.4g

Smoky Roasted Vegetables

Serves: 8
Prep Time: 1 hour 40 mins
Thin slices of the summer vegetables are baked together with herbs to make this delightful dish.

Ingredients

- 2 small red onions, sliced into rounds and separated
- 1 small orange bell pepper, sliced
- 1 small summer squash, cut into 3-inch sticks
- 1 teaspoon sea salt, divided
- 1 bay leaf
- ⅓ cup extra-virgin olive oil
- 1 tablespoon red-wine vinegar
- 3 medium tomatoes, sliced
- 1 small eggplant, cut into 3-inch sticks
- 1 small yellow bell pepper, sliced
- 1 small zucchini, cut into 3-inch sticks
- 3 sprigs fresh parsley
- 2 sprigs fresh thyme
- 4 cloves garlic, divided
- 1 tablespoon balsamic vinegar

Directions

1. Preheat the oven to 350 degrees F and grease a baking dish.
2. Season vegetables with salt and transfer to the baking dish.
3. Tie parsley, thyme, and bay leaf with a kitchen string, and place them at the center of the vegetables.
4. Top with garlic cloves and some oil and bake for about 1 hour and 15 minutes.
5. Drizzle with vinegar and serve.

Nutrition

Calories: 231 Carbs: 19.6g Fats: 17.5g Proteins: 3.6g Sodium: 482mg Sugar: 10.6g

Baked Goat Cheese with Tomato Sauce

Serves: 4
Prep Time: 30 mins

This baked goat cheese with tomato sauce instantly turns your platter into a health booster.

Ingredients

- ½ cup white onions, finely chopped
- 1¼ tablespoons fresh basil, chopped
- 1½ teaspoons white wine vinegar
- ½ teaspoon kosher salt

- 4 ounces goat cheese
- 1 tablespoon olive oil
- 2 medium garlic cloves, pressed or minced
- ¼ teaspoon red pepper flakes
- ¼ teaspoon dried oregano
- 1 can (15 ounces) crushed tomatoes
- Black pepper, to taste

Directions
1. Preheat the oven to 375 degrees F and grease 4 ramekins.
2. Heat olive oil in a pan and add onions.
3. Sauté for about 3 minutes and add garlic, basil, red pepper flakes, and oregano.
4. Sauté for about 1 minute and add white wine vinegar, tomatoes, salt, and black pepper.
5. Lower the heat, cover and allow to simmer for about 10 minutes.
6. Divide this mixture into the ramekins and top with goat cheese.
7. Transfer into the oven and bake for about 15 minutes.
8. Top with basil and olive oil to serve.

Nutrition
Calories: 398 Carbs: 11.3g Fats: 15.1g Proteins: 7.3g Sodium: 258mg Sugar: 5.2g

Charred Green Beans with Mustard

Serves: 4
Prep Time: 20 mins
This delightful combination of green beans and mustard pleases the one who eats it.

Ingredients
- 3 tablespoons extra-virgin olive oil, divided
- 2 teaspoons whole-grain mustard
- 1 pound green beans, trimmed
- 1 tablespoon red-wine vinegar
- ¼ teaspoon salt
- ¼ cup toasted hazelnuts, chopped
- ¼ teaspoon black pepper

Directions
1. Preheat a grill on high heat.
2. Mix green beans with 1 tablespoon of olive oil in a pan.
3. Transfer to the grill and grill the beans for about 7 minutes.
4. Mix the beans with mustard, oil, vinegar, salt, and black pepper.
5. Garnish with hazelnuts and serve hot.

Nutrition
Calories: 181
Carbs: 8.5g
Fats: 14.6g
Proteins: 2.8g
Sodium: 348mg
Sugar: 2.4g

Chicken Recipes

Mediterranean Chicken and Orzo

Serves: 4
Prep Time: 2 hours 40 mins
All the flavors are perfectly infused into the chicken with a special herb de Provence spice mixture.

Ingredients
- 1 cup low-sodium chicken broth
- 1 medium onion, halved and sliced
- 1 pound boneless, skinless chicken breasts, trimmed
- 2 medium tomatoes, chopped
- 1 lemon, zested and juiced
- ½ teaspoon salt
- ¾ cup whole wheat orzo
- 2 tablespoons fresh parsley, chopped
- 1 teaspoon herbs de Provence
- ½ teaspoon black pepper
- ⅓ cup black olives, quartered

Directions
1. Put chicken, tomatoes, onion, lemon zest, juice, broth, salt, black pepper, and herbs de Provence in a slow cooker.

2. Cover the lid and cook on High for about 2 hours.
3. Mix well and add orzo and olives to the dish.
4. Allow it to cook for about 30 more minutes more on High.
5. Garnish with parsley and serve warm.

Nutrition
Calories: 293 Carbs: 15.1g Fats: 10g Proteins: 35.6g Sodium: 509mg Sugar: 3.2g

Greek Chicken with Roasted Spring Vegetables

Serves: 4
Prep Time: 20 mins
The crisp and crunch of this Greek chicken with roasted spring vegetables recipe has no parallel.

Ingredients
- 1 tablespoon olive oil
- ½ teaspoon honey
- ¼ cup light mayonnaise
- 1 lemon
- 1 tablespoon feta cheese, crumbled
- 2 (8 ounces) chicken breast, cut in half lengthwise
- 6 garlic cloves, minced
- ½ cup panko bread crumbs
- ½ teaspoon salt
- 2 cups (1-inch pieces) asparagus
- 1½ cups tomatoes, chopped
- Fresh dill, snipped
- 3 tablespoons Parmesan cheese, grated
- ½ teaspoon black pepper
- 1½ cups fresh cremini mushrooms, sliced
- 1 tablespoon olive oil

Directions
1. Preheat the oven to 470 degrees F and grease a baking pan.
2. Flatten the chicken pieces in a plastic wrap with a mallet.
3. Season with mayonnaise and 2 garlic cloves.
4. Mix bread crumbs with salt, black pepper and cheese in a bowl.
5. Dip the seasoned chicken into the crumbs mixture to coat well.
6. Transfer the pieces to the baking sheet and bake for about 20 minutes, flipping once in between.
7. Sauté remaining garlic with oil, salt and black pepper in a saucepan.

8. Cook for about 1 minute and add tomatoes.
9. Cook for about 5 minutes and stir in mushrooms and asparagus.
10. Toss the chicken into the saucy asparagus and serve warm.

Nutrition
Calories: 441 Carbs: 26g Fats: 20g Proteins: 41.5g Sodium: 833mg Sugar: 7.4g

Chicken with Tomato Sauce

Serves: 4
Prep Time: 25 mins
The main specialty of this chicken recipe is the balsamic tomato sauce that enhances its taste.

Ingredients
- ½ teaspoon salt, divided
- 2 (8-ounce) chicken breasts, boneless and skinless, sliced into 4 equal sized pieces
- ½ teaspoon black pepper, divided
- 3 tablespoons olive oil, divided
- 2 tablespoons shallots, sliced
- ¼ cup balsamic vinegar
- 1 tablespoon garlic, minced
- 1 tablespoon butter
- ¼ cup white whole-wheat flour
- ½ cup cherry tomatoes, halved
- 1 cup low-sodium chicken broth
- 1 tablespoon fennel seeds, toasted and lightly crushed

Directions
1. Season the chicken pieces with salt and black pepper.
2. Spread flour in a dish and dredge the chicken through it.
3. Shake off the excess flour and keep aside.
4. Heat 2 tablespoons of cooking oil in a large skillet and add 2 pieces of chicken at a time.
5. Sear for about 3 minutes on each side and transfer this chicken to a plate.
6. Cover with a foil and heat the remaining oil in the same pan.
7. Add tomatoes and shallots and cook for about 2 minutes until soft.
8. Pour in the vinegar and cook for about 45 seconds.
9. Add broth, garlic, fennel seeds, salt and black pepper and cook for about 5 minutes.
10. Stir in the butter and serve warm.

Nutrition
Calories: 304
Carbs: 9.4g
Fats: 19.2g
Proteins: 23.4g
Sodium: 107mg
Sugar: 1.1g

Hasselback Caprese Chicken

Serves: 4
Prep Time: 35 mins
This Hasselback Caprese Chicken has lots of proteins and fats in a single serving.

Ingredients
- ½ teaspoon salt, divided
- 3 ounces fresh mozzarella, halved and sliced
- 2 chicken breasts, boneless and skinless
- ½ teaspoon black pepper, divided
- 1 medium tomato, sliced
- ¼ cup prepared pesto
- 2 tablespoons extra-virgin olive oil
- 8 cups broccoli florets

Directions
1. Preheat the oven to 370 degrees F and grease a baking sheet.
2. Season the chicken with salt and black pepper.
3. Insert mozzarella and tomato slices in the chicken cuts.
4. Brush with pesto and transfer the chicken breasts on the baking sheet.
5. Toss broccoli with oil, salt and black pepper in a large bowl.
6. Spread the broccoli mixture around the chicken and bake for about 25 minutes.
7. Dish out and serve warm.

Nutrition
Calories: 309
Carbs: 2.4g
Fats: 15.6g
Proteins: 38.9g
Sodium: 502mg
Sugar: 0.8g

Mediterranean Chicken Quinoa Bowl

Serves: 4
Prep Time: 25 mins

This is a light and healthy Mediterranean meal for everyone struggling against obesity or weight gain.

Ingredients
- ¼ teaspoon salt
- ¼ cup slivered almonds
- 1 small garlic clove, crushed
- 1-pound boneless, skinless chicken breasts, trimmed
- ¼ teaspoon black pepper
- 1 (7-ounce) jar roasted red peppers, rinsed
- 4 tablespoons extra-virgin olive oil, divided
- 1 teaspoon paprika
- ¼ teaspoon crushed red pepper
- ¼ cup pitted Kalamata olives, chopped
- 1 cup cucumber, diced
- 2 tablespoons fresh parsley, finely chopped
- ½ teaspoon ground cumin
- 2 cups cooked quinoa
- ¼ cup red onions, finely chopped
- ¼ cup feta cheese, crumbled

Directions
1. Preheat the oven on broiler setting and grease a baking sheet.
2. Season the chicken with salt and black pepper.
3. Transfer it on the baking sheet and broil for about 15 minutes.
4. Allow the chicken to cool for 5 minutes and transfer it to a cutting board.
5. Shred the chicken and keep aside.
6. Blend almonds, paprika, black pepper, garlic, 1 tablespoon of oil, red pepper, and cumin in a blender.
7. Toss quinoa, red onions, 2 tablespoons oil, quinoa, and olives in a bowl.
8. Divide the quinoa mixture in the serving bowls and top with cucumber, red pepper sauce, and shredded chicken.
9. Garnish with feta cheese and parsley to serve.

Nutrition
Calories: 741
Carbs: 62.1g
Fats: 33.7g
Proteins: 48.4g
Sodium: 548mg
Sugar: 3.6g

Olive Chicken

Serves: 6
Prep Time: 45 mins
An aromatic blend of chicken juices and tomatoes mixed sauce in which the chicken is cooked and topped with olives.

Ingredients
- 2 tablespoons white wine
- 3 garlic cloves, minced
- 2 teaspoons olive oil
- 6 chicken breast halves, skinless and boneless
- ½ cup onions, diced
- ½ cup white wine
- 1 tablespoon fresh basil, chopped
- 2 fennel bulbs, sliced in half
- Salt and black pepper, to taste
- 3 cups tomatoes, chopped
- 2 teaspoons fresh thyme, chopped
- ½ cup kalamata olives
- ¼ cup fresh parsley, chopped

Directions
1. Heat oil with 2 tablespoons white wine in a large skillet on medium heat.
2. Add chicken and cook for about 6 minutes per side.
3. Transfer the chicken to a plate and stir in garlic.
4. Sauté for about 30 seconds and add onions.
5. Sauté for about 3 minutes and stir in fennel and tomatoes.
6. Allow it to boil and lower the heat.
7. Add half cup white wine and cook for about 10 minutes.
8. Stir in basil and thyme and cook for about 5 minutes.
9. Return the cooked chicken to the skillet.
10. Cover the cooking pan and cook on low heat.
11. Stir in parsley and olives and cook for about 1 minute.

12. Adjust seasoning with salt and black pepper to serve.

Nutrition
Calories: 428
Carbs: 6.1g
Fats: 13.7g
Proteins: 67.9g
Sodium: 211mg
Sugar: 2.9g

Roasted Mediterranean Chicken

Serves: 4
Prep Time: 55 mins
Roasted Mediterranean chicken always sounds delicious when you plan a festive dinner.

Ingredients
- 1 tablespoon fresh oregano
- 1 teaspoon fresh rosemary, chopped
- 1½ pounds chicken thighs, boneless and skinless
- 1 red onion, sliced
- 2 garlic cloves, minced
- 1-pound asparagus spears, trimmed and cut
- 1 cup cherry tomatoes, diced
- 2 tablespoons balsamic vinegar
- 2 tablespoons fresh parsley, chopped
- 1 tablespoon fresh basil, chopped
- ¼ teaspoon salt
- ¼ teaspoon black pepper
- 8 oz. mushrooms, diced
- ½ cup green bell pepper, chopped
- 1 tablespoon olive oil
- 1 (16 ounces) can cannellini beans
- 10 pitted kalamata olives, sliced

Directions
1. Preheat the oven to 425 degrees F and grease a baking pan
2. Mix rosemary, oregano, basil, salt, pepper, and parsley in a bowl.
3. Place the chicken in the baking pan and season with herbs mixture.
4. Toss mushrooms with garlic, bell pepper, onions and oil.

5. Add this mixture to the pan around the chicken and roast for about 30 minutes.
6. Add asparagus, beans, tomatoes, olives and balsamic vinegar and basil mixture to the chicken pans.
7. Bake for 15 minutes and dish out to serve warm.

Nutrition
Calories: 498
Carbs: 52.7g
Fats: 8.6g
Proteins: 56.1g
Sodium: 497mg
Sugar: 4.4g

Lemon-Thyme Chicken

Serves: 4
Prep Time: 30 mins
It is a nice party meal loved for its potato fingerlings and baked with seasoned chicken.

Ingredients
- 1 teaspoon crushed dried thyme, divided
- ¼ teaspoon black pepper
- 4 small skinless, boneless chicken breast halves
- 1 lemon, thinly sliced
- 4 teaspoons extra-virgin olive oil, divided
- ½ teaspoon salt
- 1-pound fingerling potatoes halved lengthwise
- 2 garlic cloves, minced

Directions
1. Heat 2 teaspoons of oil in a skillet over medium heat and add ½ teaspoon thyme, potatoes, salt, and black pepper.
2. Cook for about 1 minute and cook, covered for about 12 minutes, stirring occasionally.
3. Push the potatoes to a side and add rest of the oil and chicken.
4. Sear the chicken pieces for 5 minutes on each side and sprinkle with thyme.
5. Arrange lemon slices over the chicken and cover the pan again.
6. Cook for about 10 minutes and dish out to serve warm.

Nutrition
Calories: 483
Carbs: 18.8g
Fats: 9.4g
Proteins: 80.3g
Sodium: 523mg
Sugar: 1.2g

Mediterranean Chicken with Potatoes

Serves: 6
Prep Time: 50 mins

This juicy chicken and pan-cooked vegetables combination is hard to resist for anyone.

Ingredients
- 1 tablespoon olive oil
- ¼ teaspoon dried thyme
- 12 small red potatoes, halved
- 4 teaspoons garlic, minced and divided
- 1 teaspoon salt, divided
- ½ teaspoon black pepper, divided
- 2 pounds chicken breast, cut into bite-sized pieces
- ¾ cup dry white wine
- ½ cup pepperoncini peppers, chopped
- 2 cups plum tomatoes, chopped
- 1 (14-ounce) can artichoke hearts, quartered
- 3 thyme sprigs
- 1 cup red onion, sliced
- ¾ cup chicken broth
- ¼ cup pitted kalamata olives, halved
- 2 tablespoons fresh basil, chopped
- ½ cup fresh Parmesan cheese, grated

Directions
1. Preheat the oven to 400 degrees F and grease a baking sheet.
2. Toss garlic, salt, oil, thyme, potatoes, and black pepper in a bowl.
3. Transfer to a baking sheet and bake for about 30 minutes.
4. Grease a Dutch oven with cooking spray and warm it over medium heat.
5. Season the chicken with salt and black pepper.
6. Sear this chicken for 5 minutes on each side.
7. Cook the chicken in two batches and transfer the chicken into a plate.

8. Add onions to the same pan and stir in wine.
9. Deglaze the pan and cook the mixture until reduced to 1/3.
10. Add broth, chicken, potatoes, pepperoncini and olives.
11. Sauté for about 3 minutes and add salt, basil, garlic, artichokes, and tomatoes.
12. Cook for another 3 minutes and garnish with thyme sprigs and cheese to serve.

Nutrition
Calories: 534
Carbs: 66.8g
Fats: 9.1g
Proteins: 43.8g
Sodium: 701mg
Sugar: 6.3g

Meat Recipes

Mediterranean Beef Pinwheels

Serves: 4
Prep Time: 1 hour
Mediterranean beef pinwheel, stuffed with a layer of spinach and cheese is a charm for every dinner table.

Ingredients
- 1/3 cup lemon juice
- 2 tablespoons dried oregano leaves
- 2 pounds beef Flank Steak
- 2 tablespoons vegetable oil
- 1/3 cup olive tapenade
- ¼ cup low-fat feta cheese, crumbled
- ½ teaspoon salt
- 1 cup frozen spinach, chopped
- 4 cups cherry tomatoes

Directions
1. Preheat the oven to 420 degrees F and grease a baking dish.
2. Mix together lemon juice, oregano leaves, vegetable oil and salt in a bowl.
3. Place the steak in a baking pan and pour this mixture over it.
4. Refrigerate the steak for about 4 hours to marinate well.

5. Remove the steak from the marinade and transfer to a cutting board.
6. Drizzle the steak with olive tapenade and top with feta and spinach.
7. Roll the steak and tie with a kitchen string at different intervals.
8. Slice the steak roll cross-sectionally into equal pieces and transfer into the baking dish.
9. Pour the remaining marinade over the slices and bake for about 35 minutes.
10. Dish out and serve warm.

Nutrition
Calories: 243
Carbs: 64.2g
Fats: 64.2g
Proteins: 27.5g
Sodium: 987mg
Sugar: 7.9g

Pork Tenderloin with Orzo

Serves: 4
Prep Time: 15 mins
This recipe becomes irresistible for all when seared tenderloin is served with nicely cooked orzo pasta.

Ingredients
- 1 teaspoon black pepper, coarsely ground
- 1¼ cups orzo pasta, uncooked
- 1 package (6 ounces) fresh baby spinach
- ¾ cup feta cheese, crumbled
- 1½ pounds pork tenderloin, cubed
- 2 tablespoons olive oil
- 3 quarts water
- ¼ teaspoon salt
- 1 cup grape tomatoes, halved

Directions
1. Season the pork cubes with black pepper.
2. Heat oil in a skillet on medium heat and add seasoned pork.
3. Sear for about 10 minutes until brown and keep aside.
4. Meanwhile, boil the water in a Dutch oven and add salt and orzo.
5. Cook for about 8 minutes and stir in spinach.
6. Cook for about 1 more minute and drain it.
7. Mix the pork, tomatoes, feta cheese and remaining ingredients in a pan.

8. Add the drained orzo and mix gently to serve.

Nutrition
Calories: 683
Carbs: 74.5g
Fats: 20.2g
Proteins: 49.8g
Sodium: 616mg
Sugar: 2.5g

Vegetables Lamb Shanks

Serves: 6
Prep Time: 3 hours
Try this lamb shanks recipe to add more colors to your Mediterranean platter, which is a complete package of proteins, minerals, and vitamins.

Ingredients For Spice Mix
- 1 teaspoon sweet Spanish paprika
- 2¼ teaspoons garlic powder
- 1 teaspoon salt
- ¾ teaspoon nutmeg, ground
- 1 teaspoon black pepper

For Lamb
- 2 tablespoons olive oil
- 2 celery ribs, chopped
- 1 pound baby potatoes, scrubbed
- 3 cups low-sodium beef broth
- 2 cinnamon sticks
- 2 sprigs fresh rosemary
- 6 Lamb shanks
- 1 medium yellow onion, roughly chopped
- 3 large carrots, peeled and diced
- 2 cups dry red wine
- 1 (28-oz) can peeled tomatoes
- 4 sprigs fresh thyme

Directions
1. Preheat the oven to 350 degrees F.
2. Mix together all the spices in a bowl and rub this mixture over the lamb.
3. Heat 2 tablespoons oil in a Dutch oven on medium-high heat and add the shanks.

4. Sear for about 8 minutes per side and add carrots, onions, potatoes, and celery.
5. Sauté for about 7 minutes and stir in the red wine.
6. Deglaze the pot and add cinnamon, tomatoes, thyme, rosemary, and broth.
7. Turn off the heat after 10 minutes of cooking and cover the Dutch oven.
8. Place this covered Dutch oven in the preheated oven and bake for about 2 hours 30 minutes.
9. Dish out and serve warm.

Nutrition
Calories: 369
Carbs: 1.7g
Fats: 18.9g
Proteins: 46.2g
Sodium: 102mg
Sugar: 0.2g

Greek Beef Steak and Hummus Plate

Serves: 4
Prep Time: 25 mins
This beef steak recipe will entice you by its taste, and aroma if you enjoy Romesco every now and then.

Ingredients
- ¼ cup fresh oregano leaves, chopped
- 1 tablespoon plus 1 teaspoon garlic, minced
- 1 medium cucumber, thinly sliced
- ¼ teaspoon black pepper
- 1 cup hummus
- 1-pound beef sirloin steaks, boneless, cut 1 inch thick
- 1 tablespoon lemon peel, grated
- 1 teaspoon black pepper
- 3 tablespoons fresh lemon juice
- 2 tablespoons Romesco Sauce

Directions
1. Preheat a grill on medium heat and grease a grill grate.
2. Mix together all the dry spices and rub on both sides of the beef steaks.
3. Grill the steaks for about 15 minutes.
4. Combine sliced cucumber, lemon juice and black pepper in a bowl.
5. Slice the grilled steak and season with salt, and black pepper.

6. Serve with Romesco sauce, cucumber strips and hummus.

Nutrition
Calories: 463
Carbs: 68.7g
Fats: 37.7g
Proteins: 36.4g
Sodium: 567mg
Sugar: 19.7g

Garlic and Rosemary Mediterranean Pork Roast

Serves: 6
Prep Time: 40 mins
Garlic and rosemary Mediterranean pork roast is famous for its mild and earthy flavors.

Ingredients
- 3 garlic cloves, sliced lengthwise into slivers
- 1 teaspoon salt
- 2 tablespoons olive oil
- 2½ pounds pork sirloin roast
- Leaves of 1 sprig of fresh rosemary
- ½ teaspoon black pepper

Directions
1. Preheat the oven to 250 degrees F and grease a roasting pan.
2. Carve 12 deep slits over the pork roasts using a sharp knife.
3. Stuff these slits with garlic slivers and rosemary.
4. Season with salt and black pepper and transfer into a skillet along with olive oil.
5. Cook until brown from both the sides and transfer onto the roasting pan.
6. Place the roasting pan in the oven and bake for about 1 hour 10 minutes, flipping in between.
7. Dish out to serve.

Nutrition
Calories: 363
Carbs: 0.6g
Fats: 18.7g
Proteins: 46.1g
Sodium: 498mg
Sugar: 0g

Baked Lamb Tray

Serves: 4
Prep Time: 55 mins
This baked lamb tray is a great combination of nutrients and a perfect weekend night dinner meal to serve to your family.

Ingredients
- 1¼ cup lamb mince
- 2 onions, halved
- 2 large potatoes, cut into wedges
- 12 cherry tomatoes
- ¼ cup feta cheese, crumbled
- ¼ cup fresh white breadcrumbs
- 1 egg, beaten
- 1 large handful mint, chopped
- 2 zucchinis, cut into batons
- 2 tablespoons olive oil

Directions
1. Preheat the oven to 350 degrees F and grease a roasting pan.
2. Mix the lamb mince, crumbs, egg, onions, mint, and seasoning in a bowl.
3. Make 8 small patties out of this mixture and arrange in a roasting pan.
4. Surround with potatoes, onion wedges, zucchinis, and tomatoes.
5. Drizzle the patties with oil and seasoning and bake for about 40 minutes.
6. Garnish these patties with remaining mint and feta cheese to serve.

Nutrition
Calories: 599
Carbs: 57.1g
Fats: 28.3g
Proteins: 32.8g
Sodium: 279mg
Sugar: 16.7g

Mediterranean Beef Kofta

Serves: 4
Prep Time: 30 mins
These Mediterranean Beef Koftas taste scrumptious when served with a pesto sauce or savory mint sauce.

Ingredients
- ½ cup onions, minced
- 1-pound ground beef
- 1 tablespoon olive oil

Spices
- ½ teaspoon ground coriander
- ½ teaspoon salt
- ¼ teaspoon ground cinnamon
- ¼ teaspoon dried mint leaves
- ½ teaspoon ground cumin
- ¼ teaspoon allspice

Directions
1. Mix ground beef with spices, oil, onion and mint leaves in a large bowl.
2. Shape beef kebabs on the wooden skewers with this mixture.
3. Refrigerate these beef kebabs for about half an hour.
4. Preheat the grill and grill these kebabs for about 15 minutes, flipping constantly.
5. Remove from the grill and serve warm.

Nutrition
Calories: 216
Carbs: 1.3g
Fats: 12.2g
Proteins: 26.1g
Sodium: 152mg
Sugar: 0.3g

Blue Cheese-Topped Pork Chops

Serves: 4
Prep Time: 25 mins
These pork chops are easy to make and serve, seasoned with cayenne pepper and served with blue cheese, Italian dressing, rosemary, and tomato.

Ingredients
- 1 pinch cayenne pepper
- 2 tablespoons fat-free Italian salad dressing
- 4 (6-ounce) bone-in pork loin chops
- 1 tablespoon fresh rosemary, snipped
- ¼ cup reduced-fat blue cheese, crumbled

Directions
1. Preheat the oven at broiler settings and line a broiler tray with a foil sheet.
2. Mix the Italian salad dressing with cayenne pepper.
3. Brush both sides of the pork chops with this dressing mixture.
4. Place the pork chops on the broiler tray, and broil the pork chops for about 10 minutes, flipping in between.
5. Top the chops with cheese and rosemary to serve.

Nutrition
Calories: 506
Carbs: 3.3g
Fats: 21.6g
Proteins: 70.8g
Sodium: 246mg
Sugar: 1.6g

Lamb Pasta and Cheese

Serves: 6
Prep Time: 1 hour 50 mins
This Lamb pasta and cheese is the perfect option for you if you are looking for a rich, cheesy delight.

Ingredients
- 1 large onion, chopped
- 1 pound lean lamb mince
- 1 beef or lamb stock cube
- 14 oz. Penne pasta, boiled and drained
- ¼ cup parmesan, grated
- Garlic bread, to serve
- 1 tablespoon olive oil
- 2 garlic cloves, crushed
- 1 teaspoon ground cinnamon
- 2 (14 oz.) cans chopped tomatoes
- 1 tablespoon dried oregano
- 1¼ cups ricotta
- ¼ cup milk

Directions
1. Preheat the oven to 375 degrees F and grease a baking dish.
2. Heat oil in a medium sized skillet and add garlic and onions.

3. Sauté for about 3 minutes and add lamb mince.
4. Cook until it turns brown and add cinnamon, oregano, stock cube,s and tomatoes.
5. Cover this mixture and cook for about 10 minutes stirring occasionally.
6. Mix parmesan cheese, milk, seasoning and ricotta in a large bowl.
7. Add the macaroni and mix it with the cheese mixture.
8. Spread lamb sauce in it and top evenly with penne and cheese mixture.
9. Transfer the baking dish in the oven and bake for about 30 minutes to serve.

Nutrition
Calories: 544
Carbs: 57.9g
Fats: 21.4g
Proteins: 30.1g
Sodium: 163mg
Sugar: 4.6g

Dessert Recipes

Banana Greek Yogurt Bowl

Serves: 4
Prep Time: 10 mins
This banana Greek yogurt bowl is great to serve both as an after meal dessert or even as breakfast on the Mediterranean diet.

Ingredients
- 2 medium bananas, sliced
- 4 cups vanilla Greek yogurt
- ¼ cup creamy natural peanut butter
- 1 teaspoon nutmeg
- ¼ cup flax seed meal

Directions
1. Put yogurt in the serving bowls and stir in melted butter, flaxseeds and nutmeg.
2. Top equally with banana slices and serve immediately.

Nutrition
Calories: 414
Carbs: 48.3g
Fats: 14.7g
Proteins: 24.7g
Sodium: 143mg
Sugar: 31.7g

Greek Baklava

Serves: 12
Prep Time: 1 hour 5 mins
Baklava is especially famous in Greece and turkey, made with layers of phyllo sheets layered with a mildly sweet nut paste.

Ingredients
- 2 cups almonds, chopped
- 1 cup sesame seeds
- 1 teaspoon ground cloves
- 12 sheets phyllo pastry dough
- 2 cups walnuts, chopped
- 2 teaspoons ground cinnamon
- 3 tablespoons honey
- 1 cup extra-virgin olive oil

Syrup:
- 1¼ cups honey
- 1 lemon, peeled and juiced
- 2 cups water
- 1 cinnamon stick

Directions
1. Preheat the oven to 350 degrees F and grease a baking sheet and phyllo sheets with olive oil.
2. Mix together walnuts, almonds, cinnamon, sesame seeds, honey, and cloves in a bowl.
3. Place this layer in the baking dish and top with 3 more layers of phyllo sheets.
4. Pour in half of the nut mixture and spread it evenly.
5. Add layers of 4 oiled phyllo sheets again and pour the other half of the nut mixture on top.
6. Bake the baklawa for 35 minutes in the oven.
7. Slice the layers into squares and let it cool.
8. On the other hand, let simmer all the sauce ingredients for about 15 minutes.
9. Pour it over the baklava pieces and serve.

Nutrition
Calories: 651
Carbs: 61.3g
Fats: 43.8g
Proteins: 13g
Sodium: 149mg
Sugar: 40.1g

Popped Quinoa Bars

Serves: 6
Prep Time: 10 mins
These bars are relatively simple to make as you only need to combine everything together, and it does not involve cooking.

Ingredients
- 1 cup dry quinoa
- 4 (4 oz.) semi-sweet chocolate bars, chopped
- ½ teaspoon vanilla
- 1 tablespoon peanut butter

Directions
1. Toast quinoa in a pan until golden and stir in vanilla, chocolate, and peanut butter.
2. Spread this mixture evenly in a baking sheet and refrigerate for about 3 hours.
3. Break it into small pieces and serve to enjoy.

Nutrition
Calories: 278
Carbs: 36.2g
Fats: 11.8g
Proteins: 6.9g
Sodium: 37mg
Sugar: 15.4g

Honey yogurt cheesecake

Serves: 8
Prep Time: 1 hour 15 mins
This yummy yogurt cheesecake has a crispy amaretti biscuit crust with a yogurt and honey cheesecake filling.

Ingredients
- 3 tablespoons almonds, flaked
- 1 cup Greek yogurt
- 2 eggs
- 1 orange, zested
- Fresh fruit, to serve
- 4 oz. amaretti biscuits
- 3 tablespoons almond butter, melted
- 26 oz. mascarpone
- 1 lemon, zested
- 1 cup honey

Directions
1. Preheat the oven to 280 degrees F and grease a baking dish.
2. Seal almonds and biscuits in a ziplock bag and crush them with a rolling pin.
3. Toss this mixture with butter and crumbs and transfer evenly into a baking dish.
4. Bake for about 10 minutes and dish out.
5. Whisk eggs, yogurt and mascarpone with a beater and stir in honey, orange and lemon zest.
6. Transfer the batter to the baked crust and cover the pan with a foil tent.
7. Bake for about 1 hour and garnish with honey and almonds to serve.

Nutrition
Calories: 368
Carbs: 10g
Fats: 30g
Proteins: 17g
Sodium: 227mg
Sugar: 0.3g

Orange Sesame Cookies

Serves: 24
Prep Time: 35 mins
These orange sesame cookies, which are loved for their refreshing citrus flavor, are baked to achieve a nice, aromatic flavor.

Ingredients
- 2 cups brown sugar
- 1 lemon, juiced
- 2 cups extra virgin olive oil

- 1 cup orange juice, freshly squeezed
- 1 shot brandy
- 1 teaspoon ground cloves
- 2 teaspoons baking soda
- 1 cup sesame seed
- 1 teaspoon ground cinnamon
- 7½ cups whole wheat flour

Directions
1. Preheat the oven to 350 degrees F and grease a baking tray.
2. Beat sugar with olive oil in an electric mixer until dissolved.
3. Add orange juice and beat again for 2 minutes.
4. Stir in lemon juice, cinnamon, cloves, baking soda, and brandy.
5. Fold in the flour and mix well to prepare smooth cookie dough.
6. Make small cookies and roll them in sesame seeds.
7. Arrange the cookies on the baking tray and bake for about 25 minutes.
8. Dish out to serve and enjoy.

Nutrition
Calories: 375
Carbs: 44.5g
Fats: 20.2g
Proteins: 5.2g
Sodium: 109mg
Sugar: 5.2g

Almond Orange Pandoro

Serves: 6
Prep Time: 10 mins
Pandoro cake has a different shape, which makes this dessert a unique dish for the table.

Ingredients
- 1¼ cups mascarpone
- 1 large orange, zested
- ¼ cup almonds, whole
- 1¼ cups coconut cream
- 4 tablespoons sherry
- 1 pandoro, diced

Directions
1. Whisk cream with mascarpone, icing sugar, ¾ zest and half sherry in a bowl.
2. Place the bottom slice of pandoro in a plate and top with remaining sherry.
3. Spoon the mascarpone mixture over the slice and top with almonds.
4. Place another pandoro slice over and continue adding layers of pandoro slices and cream mixture to serve.

Nutrition
Calories: 346
Carbs: 8.5g
Fats: 10.4g
Proteins: 7.7g
Sodium: 167mg
Sugar: 2.4g

Fruity Almond cake

Serves: 8
Prep Time: 2 hours 10 mins
Try this almond cake recipe, which is ultra-spongy in texture for a chunky and soft cake bite.

Ingredients
- 2 large oranges, zested and juiced
- 1¼ cups butter, softened
- 5 oz. whole wheat flour
- 2 teaspoons mixed spice
- 5 oz. whole almond
- 2 pounds mixed dried fruit
- ½ cup sherry
- 1¼ cups light muscovado sugar
- 1 vanilla pod, seeds scraped
- 4 oz. ground almond
- 4 large eggs, beaten

Directions
1. Preheat the oven to 280 degrees F and grease a baking dish.
2. Mix fruits, sherry, orange juice and zest in a bowl and refrigerate overnight.
3. Grease a cake pan with butter and spread brown paper in it.
4. Beat sugar and vanilla seeds in butter until smooth and creamy.
5. Add spices, flour and ground almond and mix well until smooth.
6. Fold in marinated fruits and whole almonds.

7. Pour the batter in the baking dish and bake it for 1 hour 30 minutes.
8. Reduce the heat of the oven to 250 degrees F and bake for 1 hour and 30 minutes to enjoy.

Nutrition
Calories: 613
Carbs: 54.1g
Fats: 41.8g
Proteins: 9g
Sodium: 261mg
Sugar: 36.8g

Honey Glazed Pears

Serves: 3
Prep Time: 35 mins
These roasted pears with a sweet honey glaze are a perfect option if you have a taste for a fruity dessert after a meal.

Ingredients
- ¼ cup pear nectar
- 2 tablespoons almond butter
- Dollop of cream
- 3 ripe medium pears, peeled, halved and cored
- 3 tablespoons honey
- 1 teaspoon orange zest
- ½ cup mascarpone cheese
- 1/3 cup salted pistachios, roasted and chopped

Directions
1. Let your oven preheat at 4000 F (2040 C)
2. Spread the sliced pear in a baking pan with their cut sides down.
3. Pour honey, butter, nectar and orange zest on top.
4. Roast these pears for 25 mins in the preheated oven.
5. Mix sugar with mascarpone and top the baked pears with it.
6. Garnish with honey and pistachios.
7. Enjoy.

Nutrition
Calories: 349
Carbs: 53.6g
Fats: 14.3g

Proteins: 6g
Sodium: 108mg
Sugar: 41.5g

Compote Dipped Berries Mix

Serves: 4
Prep Time: 20 mins
Berry compotes are great to serve as desserts or to make more desserts out of it.

Ingredients
- 3 orange pekoe tea bags
- 1 cup fresh strawberries, hulled and halved lengthwise
- 1 cup fresh red raspberries
- ½ cup water
- 34-inch sprigs fresh mint
- 1 cup fresh golden raspberries
- 1 cup fresh blackberries
- 1 cup fresh sweet cherries, pitted and halved
- ½ cup pomegranate juice
- Fresh mint sprigs
- 1 cup fresh blueberries
- 1 ml bottle Sauvignon Blanc
- 1 teaspoon vanilla

Directions
1. Preheat the oven to 280 degrees F and grease a baking dish.
2. Soak 3 mint sprigs and tea bags in hot boiled water for 10 minutes in a covered bowl.
3. Mix together all the berries and cherries in another bowl and keep aside.
4. Stir cook wine with pomegranate juice in a saucepan.
5. Add the strained tea liquid to the saucepan.
6. Toss in the mixed berries and mix them well to serve and enjoy.

Nutrition
Calories: 356
Carbs: 89.9g
Fats: 0.8g
Proteins: 2.2g
Sodium: 10mg
Sugar: 70.8g

Printed in Great Britain
by Amazon